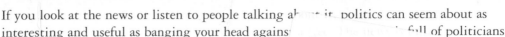

" If you look at the news or listen to people talking about it, politics can seem about as interesting and useful as banging your head against a wall. It's often full of politicians making embarrassing mistakes, or arguing about p[...] , or failing to come to an agreement about big issues such as gl[...] k: "Why bother with politics? What's it got to do with me?"

Actually, it has everything to do with you. And everyone. Almost every[...] school, even when you play a game – someone will be giving orders. At home, your parents tell you what to do. At school, it's your teachers. Sometimes, in the playground, it's simply bullies. Well, in the wider world, it's politicians.

As you get older, you will find there are lots more rules to follow. When you start to earn money, you will have to pay some to the government – and no, there's no choice! From how fast you're allowed to drive, to what day you should put your rubbish out for collection, to whether you can get money back if your mobile phone stops working – these rules will tramp around after you all your life.

Somebody makes up all these rules. But who? And by what right? The people who are in charge aren't there because they're parents or teachers, or because they're the brainiest or best. It's because they want things to change.

Half the people in the world live in a democracy. Many say that this is the best form of government, because if you don't like the rules, you can change them by voting for a different set of people to make or amend the rules in a way you agree with. But even in a democracy, millions of people have no effective voice at all. Perhaps they don't vote, or have unpopular views, or don't follow the news so simply don't know what's going on.

The truth is, politics works only when people put in the (small) amount of thinking needed to take part. It is messy, but often exciting and it's about getting the best out of what we have. If you stand up and get your point of view listened to then you are already starting to make a difference. This book will help you get there. It will tell you how it all works and how it can work for you. Some of you are the leaders of the future; others, let's hope, will be difficult to lead – asking questions, arguing back. The politics of tomorrow will be about your ideas and leadership. Do you want to get involved, or just made to follow someone else's rules? "

ANDREW MARR

CONTENTS

Who's in charge?

Government has been around for as long as there have been people to say, *"Follow me!"* Some early **tribal chiefs** would have led groups of

In *charge* of what?

In this book, we'll explore the *systems of governance* that decide who's at the top of the pile.

From the divine right of kings, to democracy, to anarchy: some government systems have shaped the *world*.

Whose *big idea* was it?

What are the ideas that drive the people who make all the *decisions?*

Do you know your **Marx** from your **Aristotle**?

So **what** can *YOU* do about all *this*?

hundreds of people. But nowadays, the decisions of presidents and prime ministers can affect literally *billions* of lives. So if there's one thing we all need to know, it's this: **who's running the show?** Because the answer to that question can make a *whole world* of difference.

How do they *stay* on top?

How do I play a *part*?

Leaders need a lot of *charisma* to keep public support – plus a lot of **cunning**, and a **little luck!**

Leaders aren't always as in control as they appear. You can have the power to change politics too.

We'll investigate how leaders keep their power, and see how the media both helps and hinders those in charge.

Find out how politics can work for you – know your rights and get involved.

If you want to make a *difference*, this book tells you how!
Find how to make **YOUR VOICE** heard, no matter how old you are.

What is politics about? When did it all start? How did we get to modern politics?

Politics evolved alongside humans. When we discovered or invented something that changed society, politics changed too.

From agriculture to ships to steam engines, discover what these politics-changing discoveries were, and see how they have influenced the world we live in today.

Do we NEED someone in charge?

IMAGINE *you and your friends are shipwrecked* on a tropical island. Sounds fun? It might be at first, but **WITHOUT** government and laws telling you what to do and when to do it, things might turn a little *nasty*.

Here's what may happen:

On a desert island somewhere in the tropics

We should ration our food, just in case we are stuck here for a while.

Some of the survivors start to throw a party...

Some time later

Hey! I need that to build a shelter!

Don't be such a spoilsport! Come and party with us.

... and arguments start over the island's resources.

A few moments later

Come down. No one will hurt you.

Yes we will. He deserves it!

Some time later

I've done everything! I should have it.

Wait a minute! I caught the fish!

... and everyone wants to deal out their own form of justice.

Soon, after several hot days, everyone is in

THE STATE OF NATURE

THOMAS HOBBES
1588–1679

Without some form of government responsible for enforcing rules and sorting out disagreements, life would be pretty miserable. The philosopher Thomas Hobbes wrote about this in his book *Leviathan*. He argued that in a lawless society – what he calls a "state of nature" – we would all have a right to everything. But rather than leading to happiness, this would result in constant conflict. A life lived under these circumstances would be "solitary, poor, nasty, brutish, and short" – not nice!

> Without anyone in charge we would all soon be caught up in a terrible war – a WAR OF ALL AGAINST ALL.

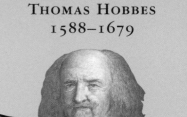

That night

This divides the group and causes more arguments.

The next day

Everyone then starts to look out for themselves...

That night

the same boat (well, on the same island).   Finally, everyone sits down to decide who's in charge!

Before you start...

The world of **politics** is full of long words and tricky definitions. To help you get started here's a breakdown of the basic *vocabulary* that will get you started on finding out **who's in charge.**

What is...
the state?

What is...
a citizen?

What is...
government?

The state is the area (or areas) of land that is under the control of a particular government. Usually, the state covers the same area as a country, and includes the people in charge, the businesses, and all the people in it.

A citizen is a person who is allowed to participate within the state. People who live and work legally in a country are known as its citizens. If you are a refugee or have illegally entered a state you aren't considered a citizen and may be thrown out.

The government is the body that runs a state. It is made up of departments that decide what is allowed to happen in the state and what isn't. There are many different types of government, which we will look at later in the book.

The word POLITICS comes from the Greek

Right or wrong?

Politics is about ideas, opinions, and people's needs. What will help one group of people may hinder another group of people. We are not going to tell you what is right or wrong because in different situations even this can differ. What we are going to show you are the facts, structures, and basics of government and politics. All with a dash of fun!

> I think my way is best and will help the most people.

> But my way will help the people who need help the most.

What is...	*If a word ends with...*	*If a word ends with...*
a politician?	**~archy**	**~ism**

A politician is someone who participates in politics. He or she is normally part of the government and their role is to advise on what is the best solution to any problems that the state may be facing. Politicians can be elected or appointed.

... or ~cracy, then it relates to a style of government. You will see many long words with these endings in this book. You may already be familiar with some, such as monarchy and democracy, but they will all be explained in chapter two.

A word that ends with ~ism is a name given to a specific set of political ideas. These will all be explained in chapter three. Here are a couple you may already know – capitalism and communism.

word *politikos*, which means *affairs of state.*

Should I STAY or should I *go*?

Over the millions of years that humankind has evolved on Earth, there have been several key events that have shaped the politics we know today. But what has politics got to do with cavemen? Everything. In Africa, politics started with the first step, as our ancestors started to walk…

> ARE WE NEARLY THERE YET?

SETTLING DOWN

Looking for food was hard work, so people decided to settle down. The invention of agriculture allowed people to live in one place and leaders had to learn how to organize settlements and solve new problems.

4.5 MILLION YEARS AGO

10,000 BCE

6000 BCE

MOVING FOOD

Politics is all about solving problems and our early ancestors had one big problem – survival! They were hunter-gatherers and had to keep on the move to find their next meal. Strong leadership was important because one bad choice could mean death!

A KING WAS BORN

As settlements grew larger they became civilizations. More people meant more problems, so new styles of leadership, or government, were needed. The Sumerian empire (southern Iraq) led the way. Known as the Cradle of Civilization, it was organized into many city-states, each with its own ruling priest-king. This was the first monarchy.

PYRAMID POWER

Once in power, the trick was to keep hold of it. The first pharaoh of Egypt, Narmer, made sure his role would pass to his son by declaring all kings to be living gods. The need to prove their power stayed with all Egyptian pharaohs. They built huge monuments, such as the Sphinx and the pyramids, demonstrating their power and authority to the citizens and scaring off would-be invaders.

ONLY THE POWERFUL CAN BUILD SUCH WONDERS!

3900 BCE   2500 BCE   1700 BCE

BORDER BATTLES

Bigger states also meant bigger borders. The earliest recorded border dispute was between the two Sumerian city-states of Umma and Lagash. The priest-king from the neutral city-state of Kish sorted the argument and established a new border by placing a pillar inscribed with his decision. But it didn't last long – the unhappy priest-king of Umma destroyed it.

TALENTED FEW

Monarchy wasn't the only type of government in use. The Minoan civilization (based in Crete, Greece) rewarded talented people with positions of power. They were a trading empire and put their best salesmen in charge of all the big decisions. This new style of government was known as aristocracy.

SOLD

Spreading influence

People settled all around the world. But that didn't mean they were happy with what they had – far from it. Growing civilizations and the desire for more power and wealth saw the emergence of land empires and, with them, new ways to rule.

VOTE HERE

FATHER OF DEMOCRACY
In around 505 BCE, Cleisthenes created the first democracy in the Greek city-state of Athens. The democracy, where any free man was allowed to vote, lasted 100 years.

640 BCE   509 BCE   505 BCE

A WEALTH OF POWER
Wealth is a sign of power. In 640 BCE, the King of Lydia (Turkey) took this to the next level when he ordered the first coins to be made. They were made of electrum (a mix of gold and silver).

SENATE POWER
Changes in leadership were happening all over Europe. In 509 BCE, the city-state of Rome became a fully-fledged republic when it ousted the ruling king, Tarquin the Proud. The senate now had power and they held yearly elections to appoint two consuls. The consuls made laws, acted as judges, and served as the head of the great Roman army.

DO YOU KNOW WHO I AM?

A GREAT EMPIRE

One way to gain more power was to gain more land. The Macedonian warlord Alexander the Great showed everyone how to do it. He led his Greek army into Africa, and east through Persia into India. It was the first great land empire, though it didn't last long – Alexander died at the age of 32.

WHO'S THE GREATEST?

TRADING PLACES

Power wasn't only achieved by war and conquering land. Around 100 BCE, with the help of boats full of goods to trade, Indian influence spread quickly through the islands of Southeast Asia.

I AM IN CHARGE!

Alexander the Great (356–323 BCE)

Julius Caesar (100–44 BCE)

336 BCE   **165 BCE**   **100 BCE**   **46 BCE**

SIZE MATTERS

The bigger the state, the harder it is to rule. The Chinese realized this and created exams to educate scholars to help them out. This was the birth of what would become the civil service.

HAIL DICTATOR!

A side-effect of having power is that other people want it! The Roman empire spread across the Mediterranean and its leader, Julius Caesar, had just conquered the Gauls (France). But all was not well at home as others tried to get him out. Caesar returned home and removed the senate's power and appointed himself dictator for life.

WAY OUT

POWER struggle

Empires were growing fast and the citizens started to realize their lives weren't that great. Rulers now had to contend with local uprisings and unpleasant peasants!

THIS FIELD CAN BE YOURS — BUT ONLY IF YOU DO AS I SAY!

THANKS, KING!

WRITTEN RULES

It wasn't just land that some rulers had to give away to keep their job. In 1215, English barons forced King John to give away some powers. By signing the Magna Carta, King John agreed that no free man would be jailed or punished without legal process, and no taxes imposed without consent from the Great Council.

850 CE   1198   1215

LAND AND LOYALTY

Rulers had to keep their people loyal. From around 850 CE the monarchs of the Frankish empire (France and western Europe) bought the loyalty of the noble class by giving them land to run. This was the start of feudalism, which gave power to a weak monarch, but it enslaved the working peasants and created a class system.

INFLUENCE TRAVELS

Land wasn't the only useful tool to keep power – religion was also used to control the masses. The Catholic Church spread its influence around the world. In 1198, Lotario dei Conti di Segni became Pope Innocent III. He was so influential he could choose whom he wanted to lead the Catholic states within Europe and would isolate those that disobeyed him. He was behind the evil Inquisition and even helped organize a "holy war" against Islam – so maybe not so innocent after all.

Pope Innocent III (1160–1216)

REVOLTING PEASANTS!

Despite bribes of land and increased citizens' rights, society was unequal and many people were unhappy. When King Richard II of England imposed a new tax, the peasants held a mass protest in London. The 14-year-old king regained control, but only after tricking the peasants and killing their leader Wat Tyler.

Wat Tyler (d.1381)

DON'T LOSE YOUR HEAD!

Four hundred years after the Peasants' Revolt came the French Revolution. In 1789, King Louis XVI and the aristocracy lost their power and their heads as the French peasants rebelled. France became a constitutional monarchy, and the revolution influenced politics around the world.

1381   1492   1789

THE AGE OF EMPIRES

The middle ages was a time of social unrest in Europe, but also one of improved maritime technology. This allowed leaders to increase their powers abroad. In 1492, while looking for a trade route to India, explorer Christopher Columbus discovered the New World (South America) and claimed it for the state of Spain. The native people had little choice – they couldn't cope with the Spanish firepower. It was the dawn of the age of colonization. Soon England, France, and the Netherlands joined the Spanish in building empires.

Christopher Columbus (1451–1506)

Full STEAM ahead!

It had been proven in France that revolutions could lead to political change. But perhaps the biggest revolution of all was not brought about by unhappy people, but by machines...

WORLD UNION

Two world wars had taken their toll on the world, so in 1945 the leaders of the free world got together and decided it would be best to try to get along. Not an easy task, so they started the United Nations.

INDUSTRIAL REVOLUTION

The invention of the steam engine really got the world of politics moving. How? The Industrial Revolution in the 19th century wasn't just about making more stuff more quickly – it also brought down feudalism. It triggered changes in working conditions as labour unions were set up, and workers had leisure time to spend money and relax. For the first time in history, the citizens had a voice.

1800s

PUT YOUR HAND UP IF YOU'RE A DICTATOR.

1936–1939

1945 1947

EXTREMES DO BATTLE

By the 20th century, machines were being used for war. Two new political powers, fascism and communism, tried out their new war machines during the Spanish Civil War. Spain was used as a practice ground for World War II as German and Italian fascists joined forces with Spanish fascist parties. They secured victory and installed General Franco as dictator. His reign lasted until 1975.

General Franco (1892–1975)

INDEPENDENCE DAY

Times were a-changing after years of war. In 1947, Mahatma Gandhi helped lead India to independence from the British Empire. Using peaceful protest, he showed that people power was as great as military force. However, the handover of power wasn't totally peaceful. Arguments between Muslims and Hindus led to the creation of the Muslim state of Pakistan, separate from Hindu India.

Over the next 60 years new countries would form out of old states as Yugoslavia, Czechoslovakia, and the USSR break apart.

Mahatma Gandhi (1869–1948)

EQUALITY FIGHTS BACK

The 20th century saw much unrest, war, and change for Africa. In 1948, the nationalist South African government imposed a legalized racial segregation called apartheid. Over the next 50 years, people were grouped by the colour of their skin. The "whites" were given superior public services, and the "blacks" and "coloured" were treated as an underclass. After decades of internal resistance, and alienation from the international world, South Africa's apartheid fell. Equal democratic elections were held in 1994 and won by the African National Congress led by Nelson Mandela.

Nelson Mandela (1918–2013)

1950–1991   1994   2000s

OUT IN THE COLD

After two world wars, international politics had to deal with a new problem – superpowers with nuclear missiles. The two main superpowers at loggerheads were the capitalist USA and the communist USSR. The world was gripped with fear of an apocalyptic nuclear holocaust as both superpowers pointed missiles at each other in a political stand-off known as the Cold War. The conflict hit boiling point in 1962 with the Cuban Missile Crisis. The Cold War finally ended in 1991 with the collapse of the communist USSR.

GLOBAL FORUM

So where are we now? Two hundred years on from the Industrial Revolution we are in the middle of a computer revolution. The Internet has spread its reach across continents and with it, citizens have gained opportunities to interact on a global scale. Citizens from one state can comment on the political landscape of another. Blogging, tweeting, and social networking have given everyone a voice. Computer technology is already a key tool in elections in countries such as the USA and Estonia.

Who makes the rules in
your house? Or school?
Or football team?

Like them, the leader of a state
makes the rules and decisions
on behalf of other people.

But what kind of leader
is the head of your state?
What form of government
do they have? How can a
queen and a prime minister
both be in charge?

*Who really wields the power
where you live – and who
put them in charge in
the first place?*

I only wanted
to know who's
in charge!

To be a leader, you need to have authority.

I've got

King or queen, *prime minister* or *president...* EVERY state has a LEADER.

A sovereign had the authority to impose all sorts of rules and regulations on his or her people. This could include:

How much food you have to eat

Sovereigns decided how much land could be used for farming, and who the state traded with to get food.

The justice system

Sovereigns set the laws that must be obeyed, and the punishments that are given when they are not.

Education

A sovereign may declare that girls should not be allowed to go to school, or lower-class labourers cannot learn certain trades.

WHAT IS *SOVEREIGNTY?*

Sovereignty is the AUTHORITY to **make rules** and **run a state**. A sovereign has the *power* to make laws and the *right* to expect people to obey them. In the past, European kings and queens had **supreme power** over their citizens. Whatever laws a king made *had to be kept* by the people – and the king had the power to make sure they did. Today, when we vote people into parliament, we give them the sovereign authority to make decisions on behalf of the people.

CALIGULA (12–41 CE)

As a Roman emperor, I had the authority to appoint my horse to government! (But I didn't do it really.)

Sovereign states

Sovereignty isn't just about the authority a leader has over his or her people – it is also about a state's place in the world. This can be important when it comes to issues such as international trade. A sovereign state is one that is not under the control of any other power (although they might have control of other lands).

France

Martinique

France has had sovereignty over the island of Martinique since 1658 – even though the lands are hundreds of kilometres (miles) apart.

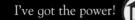

the *POWER!*

Traditionally the leader of a state was called a **SOVEREIGN**. This was just **one** person who held all the *power*. But in many countries today, sovereignty is held by a **group** of people – the *parliament*.

LAND = POWER

Sovereignty is closely connected to owning land. Landowners have the right to rule over the people who live on the land, and have control of the resources their land provides (such as oil, gold, or farm produce). Parliaments act as landowners, but a monarch (king or queen) actually owns land – usually they are the biggest landowners in their kingdom. In the past, monarchs have acquired land through marrying other royalty and combining kingdoms, or by invading another country. Explorers also claimed lands for their sovereign.

Challenging sovereignty

Not everyone agrees about who should be in control of certain lands. Countries have gone to war over it. For example, Argentina and the UK fought over sovereignty of the Falkland Islands.

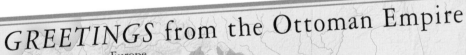

GREETINGS from the Ottoman Empire

Europe

I was here

Black Sea

Mediterranean Sea

North Africa

Middle East

An empire is a group of lands spread out across a large area that is ruled by one person. The Ottoman Empire lasted for more than 600 years, from 1299 to 1922, under the sovereignty of 36 sultans.

■ OTTOMAN EMPIRE

Africa

SULEIMAN THE MAGNIFICENT (1494–1566)

I'm the sultan, ruler of all this land. You can see I'm important just by the size of my turban.

25

TRIBAL BEGINNINGS

TRIBE 1 lives here

TRIBE 2 lives here

The first tribes lived millions of years ago.

Loyalty and leadership

Tribes were often made up of a collection of closely related families who lived and worked together. This way of life succeeded because people were loyal to each other and respected their leader (the chieftain). They trusted that he had their best interests at heart, so it made no sense to challenge his decisions. The small size of a tribe also helped tribal government to succeed. The more people there are, the harder it is to maintain loyalty.

> I am a wise and strong chieftain. My tribe is large – but the bond of kinship between my people is getting weaker.

> My tribe is small, but we are all loyal to each other.

STOP and obey!

I'M IN CHARGE!

A chieftain's main responsibilities were to defend the tribe in war, and to maintain peace and trade with neighbouring tribes. This was as well as making laws and decisions on behalf of the tribe! Who got to take on this role depended on the culture of the tribe. Some chieftains were chosen for their wisdom or strength; some for their age and experience; and some for being part of a ruling family.

Mark Fox, Chairman of the Three Affiliated Tribes

The law of the land

Modern country borders have swallowed up old tribal territories. Tribal leaders may still make the decisions that their people follow, but they must also abide by the law of the land. For example, Native American tribes in the USA are allowed to govern themselves – but like any other citizen, the members of the tribe are not allowed to break the laws of their country.

The class systems that grew out of *land*

The modern system of government is based on the idea of **TRIBES**. Before countries had definite borders, lands were *divided* into **territories**, and in each territory lived a tribe and a tribal leader. The leader was in charge: he made the rules, and there was no one above him.

FROM TRIBES TO CLASSES

Tribes were often nomadic, moving to find new pastures or better weather. Over time, they settled in one place – and that led to people owning the land. In turn, this led to a system of classes: the upper classes owned farmland, which was then the source of wealth and power. Middle classes could own houses, but no farmland. The lower classes owned no land at all.

Class rules

The idea of people belonging to different classes was as important in politics as it was in day-to-day life. In the past, rulers in many parts of the world came from the upper classes, and the king (or queen, or emperor) was the most elite of all. When kings were replaced by parliaments, nobles from the upper class made up the parliament. In most countries today, all citizens are equal and people from any class can vote or become a politician.

A world of class

Class systems have been a part of many cultures in history, although most countries today aim towards an equal, classless society.

European feudal system

Medieval feudal systems were based on the power of warfare. In Europe, knights were also nobles from the upper classes.

Japanese feudal system

In medieval Japan, there were five warrior classes, but 90% of people came from the peasant class. The lowest class were the merchants.

Indian caste system

Partly based on Hindu teachings, the highest caste (or class) was reserved for the priestly class (Brahmin).

RULER
King or emperor

UPPER CLASS
Nobles and high-ranking military

MIDDLE CLASS
Skilled workers

LOWER CLASS
Manual workers

PYRAMID OF POWER

ownership dictated WHO could be *in charge.*

Build *your own* GOVERNMENT

A *government* is a group that has CONTROL over a *state*. There are lots of *different forms* of government in the world. They are all made from the SAME BASIC PARTS, but there isn't *one set* of instructions for how they fit together.

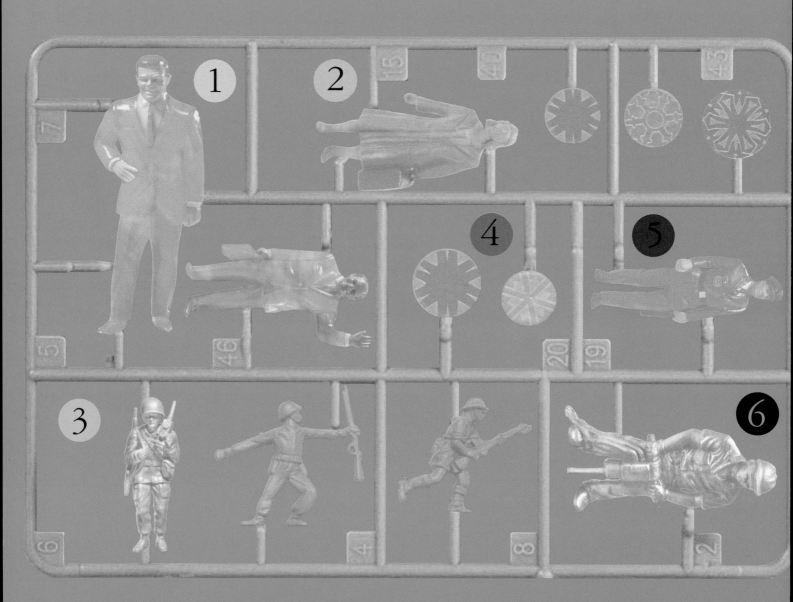

The glue that holds all the parts together is the government's politics: their *ideas and laws.*

> If I had my way, I'd do things differently...

The way a **government** *rules* a state and its citizens depends on its **structure**, **politics**, and **leader**.

> I'm in charge, and I make the big decisions.

1 LEADER
= *one that* leads *or* guides

Every group needs a leader. This person has the final say to make decisions, but also takes responsibility if things go wrong. In some forms of government the leader is called a president or prime minister, but monarchs and dictators are also leaders.

2 *Politicians*
= *people who* work in politics

No leader can work alone. A government is made up of a team of politicians whose job is to make or change a state's laws. In some governments they can take advice from experts on what's best for the state. In others, politicians follow orders from the leader.

3 ARMY
= *making sure* the state is protected

Defending a state is dangerous but essential work – otherwise other powers could take control of the land. The government is in charge of deciding when and where its army acts, basing its decisions on what is best for the state. This may include attacking other states.

4 *Money*
= *providing* the means *to* rule

Just as you need money to buy things, so does a state. Governments raise this money through taxes and use it to provide services, to trade with other states – and of course to pay their own salaries.

5 LAW *& order*
= *keeping us* under control

Law and order exists to make a state a safe place to live. A government's job is to make laws and see that they are carried out and obeyed. This is done through police and court systems, which keep order and set punishments for those who break the law.

6 *Services*
= *what the* citizens need

Health (hospitals), education (schools), and defence (army) are just some of the services that a government provides for the citizens who live in the state. It depends which country you live in as to how much help the government will provide.

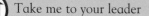

If *I* were in

... what style of government would I run? There are lots to choose from, each with its own structure and ideas. The way a government makes **decisions**, enforces **laws**, and **runs** a country all comes down to *who's* actually in charge and what they believe is *important*.

TRIBAL
We have been in charge of our own tribes for many years. Our tribal lands are within this new country, so we deserve to be in charge.

THEOCRACY
I believe that God is in charge. The state laws should be based on scriptures, which I'll interpret for you.

ARISTOCRACY
The elite should be in charge. We are the upper classes and we know what is best.

DEMOCRACY
Everyone should have the right to have a say. We will vote for the best candidate and they will listen to public opinion.

MONARCHY
I was born to be in charge. As the queen, I will do the best for my country. Then I will pass the throne onto my first-born child.

MILITARY DICTATORSHIP
I'm in charge. I have the power of the military behind me so you will do as I say.

ANARCHY
No one should be in charge! No one tells me what to do. I ain't listening to anyone... except maybe my mum.

Some types of government have had greater

CHARGE...

All types of government can be grouped into two categories. In an *AUTOCRACY,* **ONE PERSON** or a **SMALL GROUP** are in charge, often *self-appointed*. In a *DEMOCRACY,* **CITIZENS** are allowed to *have a say* in who should be in charge.

MERITOCRACY
The people in charge should be chosen on merit. The more talented and intelligent should be in charge. Like me.

GERONTOCRACY
As older people, we have the experience and wisdom to be in charge.

LOTTOCRACY
My name's come up, so it's my turn to be in charge – at least for now. The next leader will be chosen by another random lottery.

PLUTOCRACY
I'm rich! My friends and I should be in charge because we're good with money.

CORPORATOCRACY
We are the top business minds of the country. With our influence and corporate power we should be in charge.

TIMOCRACY
We own property, so are permanently connected to the country. This means we have the best interests of the land at heart.

THALASSOCRACY
Let's set sail and form a sea empire. Then we can rule the lands by controlling ports and trade.

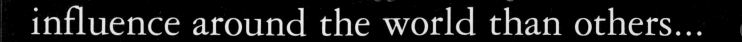

influence around the world than others...

ALL for *one*

The Greek philosopher Aristotle had *a lot* to say about POLITICS. He was especially **concerned** with a government's INTENTIONS – are they in power for themselves, or are they working for the *good of the people?*

ARISTOTLE (384–322 BCE)

MOB RULE

Aristotle said that a state is made up of the "wealthy few" and "propertyless many". For him, democracy meant "rule by the propertyless many". He didn't like democracy, saying that the poor would only have their own interests at heart and it would lead to mob rule.

number in charge + *intention*

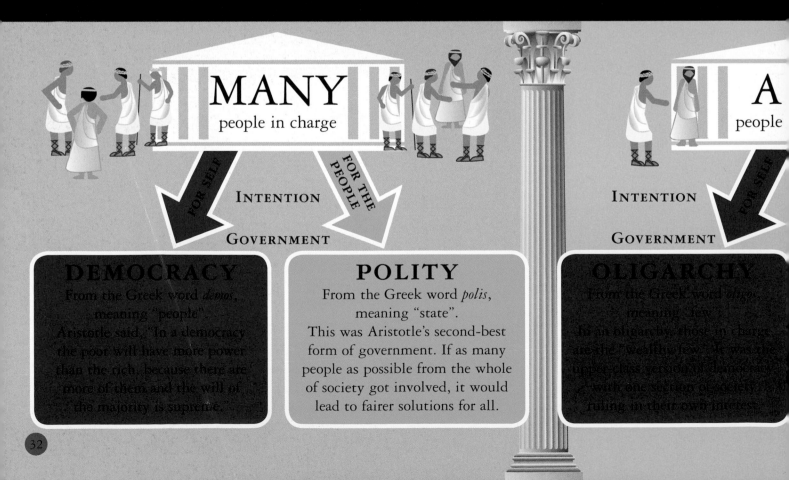

MANY
people in charge

A
people

FOR SELF

FOR THE PEOPLE

INTENTION

INTENTION

GOVERNMENT

GOVERNMENT

FOR SELF

DEMOCRACY
From the Greek word *demos*, meaning "people".
Aristotle said, "In a democracy the poor will have more power than the rich, because there are more of them, and the will of the majority is supreme."

POLITY
From the Greek word *polis*, meaning "state".
This was Aristotle's second-best form of government. If as many people as possible from the whole of society got involved, it would lead to fairer solutions for all.

OLIGARCHY
From the Greek word *oligos*, meaning "few".
In an oligarchy, those in charge are the "wealthy few". It was the upper-class version of democracy, with one section of society ruling in their own interest.

and *one* for ALL

ONE, FEW, MANY

Aristotle grouped all forms of government into three categories based on how many people were in charge. The numbers also reflected social status – the "few" were wealthy, and the "many" were poor. *The trouble was, whichever group was in charge could end up alienating the others.*

THE BEST SOLUTION

Aristotle favoured monarchy as the best form of government. One person who was clever, kind, and had the people's interests at heart would be the best ruler and law-maker. But he also recognized that this kind of person didn't come along very often!

= FORM OF GOVERNMENT

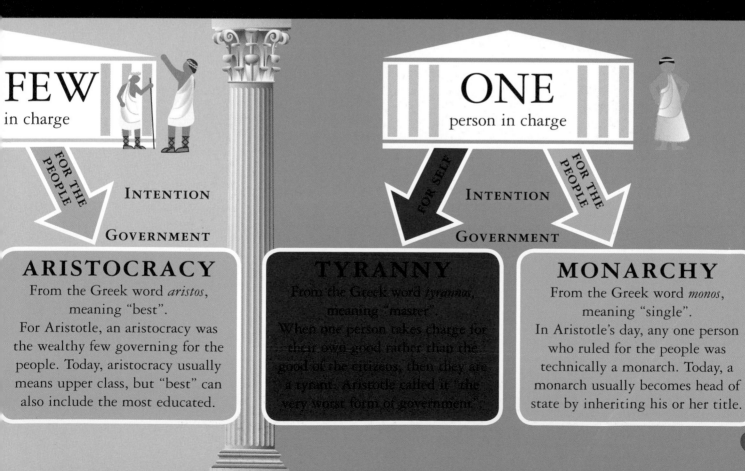

FEW
in charge

FOR THE PEOPLE

INTENTION

GOVERNMENT

ARISTOCRACY
From the Greek word *aristos*, meaning "best".
For Aristotle, an aristocracy was the wealthy few governing for the people. Today, aristocracy usually means upper class, but "best" can also include the most educated.

ONE
person in charge

FOR SELF

INTENTION

GOVERNMENT

TYRANNY
From the Greek word *tyrannos*, meaning "master".
When one person takes charge for their own good rather than the good of the citizens, then they are a tyrant. Aristotle called it "the very worst form of government".

FOR THE PEOPLE

MONARCHY
From the Greek word *monos*, meaning "single".
In Aristotle's day, any one person who ruled for the people was technically a monarch. Today, a monarch usually becomes head of state by inheriting his or her title.

What is a

Monarchy means "RULE BY
Greek words *monos* (alone,

Before parliaments, most of the world was made up of *monarchies* governed by kings and queens (or emperors, pharaohs, kaisers, or tsars). Often unelected, monarchs had unlimited power to keep their kingdom in order, which they did by leading armies into battle, acting as religious leaders, and collecting taxes.

HOW TO BECOME A MONARCH

Secrets of succession

Being a king or queen isn't a job just anyone can apply for. Monarchs usually inherit the throne from their parents, according to the "rules of succession". When a monarch dies or abdicates (resigns), power transfers to the next in line to the throne – typically the oldest son. Most monarchies run through the male line, so a son will take the throne even if he has older sisters. A family that rules for an extended period is called a dynasty.

An heir of truth

Dynasties may come to an end when a rival family challenges the throne and the reigning king is defeated in battle. The new monarch will often try to prove that they are actually the true heir to the throne. This could involve making up a new family tree and faking documents.

Of course I am the true king. Just look at my family tree – I am nothing but royalty!

Divine right

One way to stop people challenging the throne was to claim "divine right". To put an end to competing claims to the throne of England in the 17th century, James I said that God had appointed each king personally to rule. The pharaohs of ancient Egypt were seen as human incarnations of the god Horus.

I choose **YOU** to be the next king!

Kingship is one of the very best forms of government — when the king rules in the interest of the WHOLE people

monarchy?

ONE PERSON". From the single) + *archos* (ruler).

MONARCHIES TODAY

Many modern countries are constitutional monarchies. This is where the monarch has a ceremonial role as head of state, but the real power is held by elected leaders in a parliament. In the past, citizens paid tax to the monarch, but today most monarchs pay tax and are citizens of the state they are the figurehead of. Some countries have got rid of their monarchs and become republics, where all their officials are elected.

Spain, Jordan, Malaysia, Sweden, and Belgium are constitutional monarchies.

I am ABSOLUTELY the king!

In an absolute monarchy, all political power is held by a single individual. Saudi Arabia is a modern example of an absolute monarchy, where the head of state is also the head of government. King Louis XIV of France, who reigned 1643–1715, summed it up by boasting, "*L'état, c'est moi.*" ("The state, it is me.")

Saudi King and Prime Minister Salman bin Abdulaziz Al Saud

RECORD REIGNS

John I became King of France the day he was born, but he died five days later, making his reign one of the shortest in history.

King Bhumibol Adulyadej of Thailand is the world's longest serving current monarch. He came to the throne on 9th June 1946.

... But even he has some way to go to beat pharaoh Pepi II, who is said to have reigned for 94 years.

OFF with his head!

Being a monarch can have its problems. Few people dare to disagree with a king, or tell him his policies aren't working – but when all the bad feeling builds up, it can lead to revolution. King Louis XVI and his queen, Marie Antoinette, were executed in 1793, four years after the start of the French Revolution.

Aargh! I suppose this means you don't like me much then?

"But when the king rules in his *own* interest, rather than in the common interest, kingship becomes TYRANNY – and that's the very worst form of government there is." Aristotle, 384–322 BCE

As an emperor of ancient China, I am the Son of Heaven – the gods' own representative on Earth.

What is

Theocracy means "RULE Greek words *theo* (God)

A theocracy is when a state uses the BELIEFS and SCRIPTURES of a **religion** as the *basis* of its laws and decision-making. The leader works under the *guidance* and *authority* of the religion.

A HIGHER POWER

State leaders today use political systems to gain or keep power. Before these systems evolved, many leaders used religion as a source of power. Faith and superstition were used to legitimize a leader's position, especially in times of crisis.

EARLY WORSHIP

Our early ancestors used to worship the Earth and its natural forces. People had to deal with natural events they didn't understand, such as earthquakes, floods, and drought. Our ancestors would fear and respect the Earth, hoping they would survive.

RULE OF MANY

As civilizations blossomed, so did the nature of religion. Soon many powerful civilizations, such as the Egyptians, Greeks, and Romans, worshipped many gods. The people in charge used the influence and fear of the gods to confirm their position and keep hold of power.

RITUAL POWER

Several hundred years ago, South American civilizations, such as the Incas and Mayans, used ritual sacrifice in the hope the gods would help the citizens in times of crisis. Rulers would also blame problems on the gods. This way, their bad leadership wasn't noticed!

ORGANIZED POWER

The influence of organized religions has spread across and beyond borders. States would adopt one religion and follow its scriptures and writings. This led to conflict and war as state leaders used religious differences as reasons to invade or conquer other lands.

a theocracy?

BY GOD". It comes from the + *kratos* (strength, power).

THE AGE OF ENLIGHTENMENT

Religion gripped the world and its leaders for thousands of years. Rulers changed faiths to fit their desires – the Mongol leader Genghis Khan (1162–1227) tried out different religions before choosing Islam. But in the 18th century, Western philosophers and scientists started to believe that reason and science should be the foundation of a state rather than faith and religion. This period of time was known as the ENLIGHTENMENT.

SECULAR STATES

The ideas of the Enlightenment spread around many parts of the world and it was soon written into most constitutions that religious influence should be separate from the running of the state. A state that has no official religion is known as a secular state. However, this doesn't necessarily mean a ban on religion – citizens are still allowed to privately choose what religion, if any, they wish to believe in and practise.

Representing religion

There are some states that still combine religious values and scriptures with government practices and law-making. The closest thing to a theocracy that exists today is in Vatican City, where the Pope acts as leader of the state and claims sovereignty in the name of the Catholic God. The Islamic Republic of Iran also attempts to blend religion with modern structures of government. A supreme council of religious clerics guide the politics of the country while an elected president and government carry out the day-to-day runnings of the state.

"Religion is a matter which lies solely between man and his God. ... Legislature should make no law respecting an establishment of religion, or prohibiting the free exercise thereof, thus building a wall of separation between church and state."

Thomas Jefferson, third president of the USA

Pope Francis

President of Iran Hassan Rouhani

Iranian Supreme Leader Ayatollah Ali Khamenei

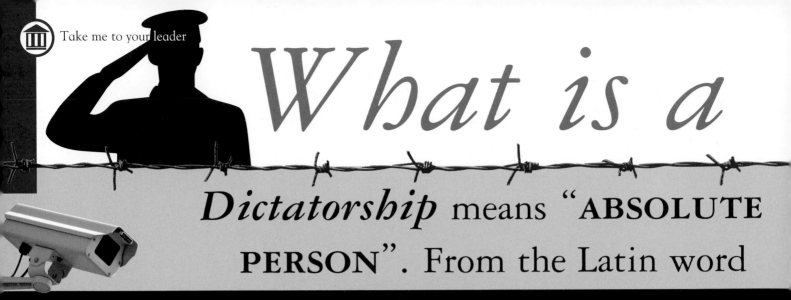

What is a

Dictatorship means "ABSOLUTE PERSON". From the Latin word

When one person has complete control over the state, then it is a *dictatorship*. A dictator holds ALL the power and sets ALL the laws. Today, dictatorships are seen as a bad form of government, but it wasn't always that way.

FROM ANCIENT ROME...

The idea of dictatorship came from ancient Rome. In emergencies, the government could give absolute power to one person for a short amount of time so they could deal with crises. In 458 BCE Rome was at war, and the government asked the farmer (and former consul, or politician) Cincinnatus to become their dictator. He took control of the army and won the war. Afterwards, the government took back the power and Cincinnatus returned to his farm.

> Well fought, centurions. Now you can help me with the harvest.

... TO MODERN TIMES

Modern dictators are not the temporary, appointed leaders they were in ancient Rome. They are known for grabbing power and using it to change the country to how they want it. Extreme dictatorships can become despotic, behaving without any consideration for the people they govern. Idi Amin was a despot, controlling Uganda from 1971 until 1979.

Idi Amin gave himself the title "His Excellency President for Life, Field Marshal Al Hadji Doctor Idi Amin, VC, DSO, MC, Lord of All the Beasts of the Earth and Fishes of the Seas, and Conqueror of the British Empire in Africa in General and Uganda in Particular".

dictatorship?

CONTROL BY ONE

dictare (to assert).

Benevolent dictator Guiseppe Garibaldi is hailed an Italian national hero for creating a unified Italy in the 19th century.

What's in a *name?*

The words "despot" and "tyrant" are sometimes used when talking about dictators. A despot is another word for an extreme dictator: a person who takes complete control. A tyrant is a ruler who is cruel and oppressive. A dictator isn't necessarily cruel. There have even been a few benevolent dictators, who seized control to make life better for everyone.

TAKING CONTROL

A dictator often comes to power by force or cunning, perhaps staging a coup d'état – a challenge that deposes (gets rid of) the government. Overthrowing an existing government, even a weak one, and taking charge of millions of citizens is a hard job for one person to do alone. In most modern dictatorships, the dictator has the support of the military. This way, most threats to the new leadership are fought off.

Saddam Hussein came to power in Iraq after a coup against his own leader in 1979.

KEEPING CONTROL

Once in power, a dictator keeps strict control in various ways. There may be a ban on people setting up political parties that oppose the dictator. Newspapers and radio and television stations must support the official state ideology, or they will be shut down. They are forbidden from reporting news items that might make the dictator look bad, or even getting old or sick. Any books or works of art that challenge government policies are banned. Even public organizations such as schools are under state control and give out propaganda so citizens are only taught what the dictator wants them to learn.

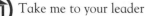

What is

Democracy means "RULE BY THE PEOPLE".
demos (people) + *kratos* (strength, power).

Democracy is different to all other forms of government because people are allowed to **VOTE** for what (*or who*) they think is *best*.

FREE TO VOTE

The first ever democratic system existed more than 2,500 years ago, in ancient Greece – but it's a different system to one we would recognize today. Each city had its own democracy, rather than there being one body governing the whole country. Any free man (one who wasn't a slave) could stand up and speak to his fellow citizens about his ideas. He was also allowed to vote. Women, children, and slaves were not allowed to stand or to vote.

> It's the same in every city – we never get a say!

There are **two main types** of democracy:

Direct democracy

In ancient Greek cities, lots of free men made speeches in the busy marketplace as a way of getting support for their ideas and views. Any free man who liked an idea could vote for it – this is direct democracy. The process still exists today, when a country asks its citizens to vote directly on an issue (this is called a referendum).

> Bah! You're talking nonsense.

> I like his ideas! I'm going to vote for him to lead us.

Representative democracy

Most democratic countries today have representative democracy, where people vote for a representative (such as a member of parliament) to vote on ideas put forward in government. While people have the power to vote someone into government, once they are in power, the people no longer have much control.

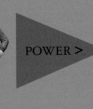

> I think you'll vote for things I agree with.

POWER >

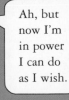

> Ah, but now I'm in power I can do as I wish.

democracy?

It comes from the Greek words

> "Government OF the people, BY the people, FOR the people."
>
> Abraham Lincoln (1809–1865), 16th president of the USA

IT'S VITAL TO VOTE

Both types of democracy need a voting system in order to work – it's how people choose what they want. Unlike monarchs or dictators, who inherit or seize power, governments and rulers (presidents and prime ministers) need to be supported and accepted by the people. If people don't like what the current government is doing, they may vote for someone else next time.

IS MODERN DEMOCRACY ACTUALLY DEMOCRATIC?

It could be argued that modern democracy isn't actually all that fair. For example, rich people and poor people are often affected in very different ways by most political decisions. Also, minority groups don't always get heard – although there are laws in place to protect the rights of minorities. So even with democracy, the outcome isn't always what is best for everyone.

POOR | RICH

Let's have a party In a democracy, people can vote for their favourite person, but it is better to vote for ideas and policies. These are usually offered by political parties, which are people with similar ideas coming together under one agenda (a list of what they will do if they are elected).

WE WANT... LESS TAX

WE WANT... MORE JOBS

WE WANT... EQUALITY

> "No one pretends that democracy is **PERFECT** or **all-wise**. *Indeed,* it has been said that democracy is the *WORST* form of government *except* all those **other forms** that have been tried from time to time."
>
> Sir Winston Churchill (1874–1965), former British Prime Minister

41

THE *tree* OF

A democratic form of government has THREE main areas where decisions are made. Each is *responsible* for one aspect in the big political picture. This is known as the **"separation of powers"**.

IDEA MAKERS

The **EXECUTIVE** comes up with ideas to make life better for the citizens, and put policies and laws into action. This group is made up of the main elected government officials, including the leader.

I think we're all in agreement on this new law. Let's take it to the Legislature and get them to vote on it!

Leader

Chancellor

Deputy

Executive

US presidents, such as Barack Obama, are elected by the people and by the Electoral College.

PRIME MINISTER OR PRESIDENT?

In a parliamentary democracy the idea makers are known as a cabinet, which is led by a prime minister. The prime minister isn't elected by the public, but by the controlling party in parliament – the party that got the most votes in the last election and holds the most seats in government. In most presidencies, the public vote directly for who they want to be president. They also vote for politicians to represent their local communities.

The WAY a government's powers are

DEMOCRACY

LAW MAKERS

The **LEGISLATURE** includes all the elected officials in parliament. They debate and vote on proposed laws. In some countries, the Legislature also holds the Executive to account (they make sure they behave!).

Charles-Louis de Secondat, Baron de Montesquieu (1689–1755)

Everyone in the parliament

> Listen up, Britain! This has been approved by the House of Commons and House of Lords. It's now law.

Legislature

WHAT KIND OF DEMOCRACY?

Half of all the people in the world today live in a democracy – though there are several different types.

Argentina is a republic. This is a form of representative democracy, where voters elect representatives into government to vote on legislation (laws).

Australia is both a federation and a parliamentary democracy. In a federation, power is shared between a central government and regional areas (states or territories).

India is the world's biggest democracy, with a population of 1.25 billion people. It is a federal republic – the central government has limited power over the regions.

LAW ENFORCERS

The **JUDICIARY** interprets and upholds the law through a system of courts. It makes sure citizens are treated fairly and that their human rights are protected. It includes some elected and some appointed roles, such as judges.

> We can overrule the Executive and Legislature because we interpret the law and all citizens live under the rule of law.

Judiciary

Lords and judges   Barrister

POWER SHARING

Some states have both prime ministers and presidents, who share out responsibilities. In India, Prime Minister Narendra Modi is the head of the government, while President Pranab Mukherjee is the head of state.

Indian Prime Minister Narendra Modi and President Pranab Mukherjee

divided is set out in a constitution.

What goes on in *there?*

THE WALLS OF POWER

Inside the main government building a lot of big decisions and important discussions take place. This is where the leader and the politicians talk about politics – all the ideas and possible solutions to problems that the state will throw up.

Problems? What problems?

The state and its citizens create many problems that need to be addressed. These can include unemployment, taxes, and health care.

What is the best solution?

There are many different political groups that believe in different approaches to government. These are looked at in this chapter.

Houses of Parliament
London, England

Destroyed by fire in 1834, the building also known as the Palace of Westminster was rebuilt by 1860.

The Beehive
Wellington, New Zealand

The Beehive houses the executive branch of the New Zealand government. It is ten storeys high.

The White House
Washington DC, USA

Built between 1792 and 1800, the White House is the residence and office of the President of the United States of America.

It doesn't matter how the *government* is structured, be it a democracy or a dictatorship, there is always a main government **building**. But what goes on inside these *walls of power?*

LOCATION, LOCATION, LOCATION

Most government buildings are located in the capital city of the state. In a democracy, each branch of power has its own impressive building. Government also consists of ministries. These buildings deal with specific areas of the state, like foreign affairs, state defence, and the treasury.

I can hear a lot of arguing!

Not everyone will agree on the correct way of doing things. This arguing is called debating, which is important because it means all possible views are considered before a decision is made.

The leader and politicians work inside the building. They get to decide which ideas will become law. Some governments have employees who help run the building. These are called civil servants.

Who gets to go inside?

The Kremlin
Moscow, Russia

Located between Red Square and the Moskva River, the Kremlin is the official residence of the Russian President.

Rashtrapati Bhavan
New Delhi, India

Built using 700 million bricks, Rashtrapati Bhavan is the largest residence of a Head of State in the world.

Cheong Wa Dae
Seoul, Republic of South Korea

The official residence of the South Korean President. Its name means "the Blue House", after its distinctive blue tiled roof.

How the

The **first role** of the *government* is

THE GOVERNMENT is given the right to rule the state. But the state needs *more than the government to work*. It also requires *citizens* and something called CIVIL SOCIETY.

Civil society includes all the businesses and industries that can be used by the citizen. It has to abide by the laws set out by the government, but it is not under its control. Civil society creates jobs for the citizen, and is where social clubs meet. Charities are also part of the civil society.

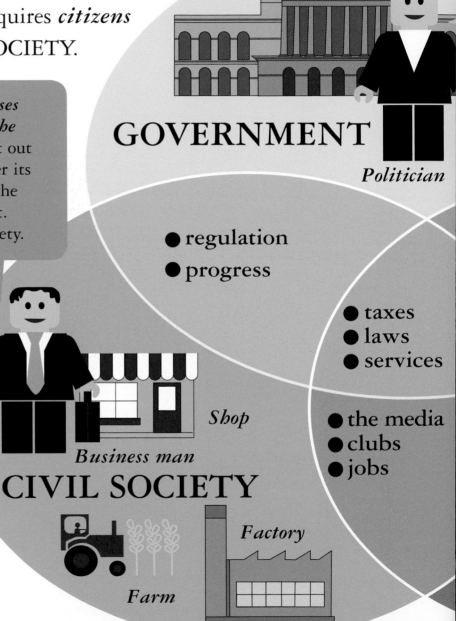

GOVERNMENT

Politician

- regulation
- progress

- taxes
- laws
- services

- the media
- clubs
- jobs

Shop

Business man

CIVIL SOCIETY

Factory

Farm

GEORG WILHELM FRIEDRICH HEGEL (1770–1831)
Hegel proposed the idea that civil society is separate to the government. Hegel believed everything in-between the government and the citizen was part of civil society. He saw it as a zone of needs and desires, where freedom and authority interacted.

Georg Hegel
German philosopher

Each zone and its components create

STATE *works*

to make sure the *state functions.*

Why the OVERLAP?

This zone includes the main government buildings and the politicians that work in them. It creates laws, collects taxes, and regulates civil society. It also sets out the rights of the citizen and offers help through welfare.

All three zones rely on each other for funding, resources, and laws. Without this cooperation the state would not work and could collapse.

- rights
- welfare
- duty

This is the zone of the citizen, and includes the home and the family. Citizens have to pay tax to fund the government, which then supplies services and gives the citizen rights. Citizens also have a duty to the state, sometimes this means helping out in a crisis.

Home

CITIZEN

AUTHORITARIANISM

This long word means "strict obedience to authority". In an AUTHORITARIAN society the government has a lot of say over what happens in civil society, and dictates what citizens do in their homes.

GOVERNMENT

CIVIL SOCIETY   CITIZEN

PINOCHET took over Chile in 1974, creating an authoritarian state. He suppressed opponents until 1990, when he finally lost power.

LIBERTARIANISM

This means more freedom. In a LIBERTARIAN society the citizen has more freedom in civil society, and the government has only a small amount of authority.

GOVERNMENT

CIVIL SOCIETY   CITIZEN

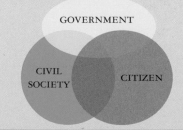

SWITZERLAND is seen as a free and neutral state. Their form of government allows for more civil freedoms.

problems for the government to solve.

51

EVERYONE has his or her own *ideas*

on how to deal with problems of the state. These opinions are known as *political ideas*, and they can all be PLOTTED across an **ideas rainbow**.

A RAINBOW OF IDEAS

The ideas rainbow shows a change in political values from an extreme left to an extreme right. The political groups that sit near each other on the rainbow hold similar ideals. A group positioned opposite will have opposing ideas.

LEFT VALUES

FREEDOM
The citizen should have more freedom in the state.

EQUALITY
Everyone has an equal right to improve.

PROGRESS
The state should change and improve.

TOGETHERNESS
Cooperation is key to the success of the state.

The IDEAS

LIBERAL

SOCIALISM
The socialist left believe in a free society that works together to improve the state.

Democratic

- - - - - - - -

Autocratic

EXTREME LEFT

COMMUNISM

Communism believes everyone should be equal, removing the elite and the class system. Everyone must help the state and participate equally. This requires a lot of authority and strict control.

Fidel Castro took over Cuba in 1959 and formed a communist state.

MANY GOVERNMENTS
have a seating plan that mirrors the RAINBOW.

RAINBOW

It started with a REVOLUTION

Why LEFT and RIGHT? It began after the French Revolution in 1789. When the new government sat down, the victorious revolutionaries sat on the left side of the chamber, and remnants of the defeated nobility sat on the right.

Where you sit defines your political values.

LIBERALISM

Liberals believe everyone is individual and we all have the right to pursue our own goals. Liberalism formed the basis of modern democracy.

MIDDLE

CONSERVATISM

The conservative right believes that longstanding tradition and hierarchy are key to running a better state.

Democratic

- - - - - - - - - - -

Autocratic

EXTREME RIGHT

FASCISM

RIGHT VALUES

AUTHORITY
The state should have more control over the citizen.

HIERARCHY
Everyone has a place in society – high or low.

TRADITION
Society is built on longstanding values.

DUTY
Everyone has a duty to help the state.

AN EASTERN VIEW

In Asian politics there is less of a rainbow. Instead the political ideas are based on strong family values, like wisdom, experience, and tradition. It delivers stern and supportive ideas that seek to achieve social harmony and emphasize individual responsibility.

Mussolini led a fascist Italy during World War II.

The big ideas

SOCIALIST PARTIES

They are many socialist and social democratic parties around the world. Here are a few examples.

 UK
The Labour Party

 USA
Democratic Party

 CANADA
New Democratic Party

 MEXICO
Party of the Democratic Revolution

 ARGENTINA
Justicialist Party

 FRANCE
The Socialist Party

 JAPAN
Democratic Party of Japan

 INDIA
Indian National Congress

 RUSSIA
A Just Russia

 AUSTRALIA
Australian Labor Party

 CHINA
China Democratic League

 GERMANY
Social Democratic Party of Germany

 SOUTH AFRICA
African National Congress

Left OR

The two political movements that dominate governments around the world are **SOCIALISM** and **CONSERVATISM**. They sit in the

SOCIALISM

SOCIALISTS believe we are **social creatures** and should be allowed to be part of an *equal community*. A socialist society is based on *cooperation* rather than *competition*.

 FREEDOM – Socialists aspire for social freedom that gives everyone the same opportunities. They believe society should be free to change, and the state's resources should be divided equally between the citizens.

 EQUALITY– Justice and fairness are central to socialism. Socialists believe society should be a "level playing field" that allows everyone the same opportunity to succeed and better themselves.

 ECONOMY – Socialists believe the state should own and benefit from the success of key industries and businesses. Social democrats believe in capitalism, but only if it works for everyone, not just the already rich.

SOCIETY – Socialists believe in community spirit. Socialists want everyone to work together for a common purpose and a better society. They prefer cooperation over competition.

SOCIALISM comes from the Latin *"sociare"* = to SHARE *or* COMBINE.

EGALITARIANISM
is a belief that **equality** should be the main focus of *politics and society.*

54

RIGHT?

democratic area of the ideas rainbow. Their beliefs in how the government, society, and the citizen should interact are very different.

CONSERVATISM

CONSERVATIVES look to **conserve** what is already in place and *try to avoid change* and reform. **Tradition** and **hierarchy** are key elements of conservatism, as well as *private ownership* and *dutiful citizens.*

AUTHORITY– Conservatives believe in authority, order, and tradition. They think that a government's authority and control is important for a stable state and community.

HIERARCHY– Conservatives think there is a natural hierarchy to human society, and that some citizens, by nature, are better off than others. They think it is the individual's responsibility to better themselves.

ECONOMY– Conservatives believe in the private ownership of all businesses and industries. They believe in capitalism, and that everyone has the right to make profit and benefit from a free market.

SOCIETY– At the heart of a conservative society are tradition, order, and duty. Conservatives look to conserve what has already been established, and believe citizens seek security in traditional values.

CONSERVATISM comes from the verb "conserve" = to KEEP *in a* STATE OF SAFETY.

NATIONALISM
is the belief that **heritage** and **traditions of the state** should be the main *focus of government.*

CONSERVATIVE PARTIES

There are many conservative political parties around the globe. Here are a few examples.

UK
The Conservative Party

USA
Republican Party

CANADA
Conservative Party of Canada

MEXICO
National Action Party

ARGENTINA
Republican Proposal

FRANCE
Union for a Popular Movement

JAPAN
Liberal Democratic Party

INDIA
Bharatiya Janata Party

RUSSIA
United Russia

AUSTRALIA
Liberal Party of Australia

CHINA
Revolutionary Committee of the Kuomintang

GERMANY
Christian Democratic Union of Germany

SOUTH AFRICA
The Democratic Alliance

Buy? SELL... INVEST!

A government has to make sure its citizens have enough food and clothes, and somewhere to live. But this can be a lot of work, so instead of giving citizens everything they need, the government can choose to be capitalist. This puts the responsibility in the hands of the citizen. They have to earn money to eat, keep warm, and stay dry.

THE AIM OF THE GAME

The goal of capitalism is to generate your own money. This can be achieved by working hard and getting a regular salary at a company, or by setting up your own business. The state allows you to do what you want with your own money. But watch out – lose it all and you won't get much help from the government!

WHAT IS CAPITALISM?

CAPITALISM is a system that encourages citizens to make as much money as possible from their hard work, skill, and opportunities. This helps the industries of the state run themselves with little interference from the government. Also if citizens make lots of money then the government can collect some (as taxes) and pay for state improvements and services.

ALL AGAINST ALL

Capitalism can sound like a good idea, but there are some bad points. First, you aren't the only citizen out to make money – everyone is. Also, the more money you start with the more opportunity you have to make more – though there are no guarantees, people can lose money as quickly as they earn it!

STATE OF MONEY

Capitalism gives the government the chance to make money out of the success of its citizens. They can impose charges on citizens, businesses, and their profits. These are called TAXES. The taxes then go into the government's pool of money to pay for services like defence, health, and education.

PRIVATE OWNERSHIP

Capitalism gives everyone the right to own their house, shop, or factory. The citizen then has the opportunity to use and improve their property so they can earn money. Ownership of property also means the citizen is linked to the land and is an active part of the state.

FREE MARKET

Unfortunately, this doesn't mean everything is free. A free market is when citizens are free to invest, save, and use their money how they wish. The free market was born out of the *laissez-faire* values of 19th century France. *Laissez-faire* means "leave it be", which the government did – they only enforced law and order. The free market is open to anyone to pursue the capitalist dream, though it is a lot easier to succeed if you already have money! Capitalism can create a divide between groups of citizens, especially between the wealthy and the poor.

REGULATION

In a free market the government will let citizens make money, but they also have to protect their citizens, so they make laws called regulations. These make it illegal to trade in certain items (such as babies and endangered animals) and make sure items are of a certain standard so citizens aren't cheated. Regulations are now commonplace, but only emerged during the 19th and 20th centuries to protect citizens, improve poor working standards, and ensure workers weren't exploited.

CAPITALISM AND POLITICS

SOCIALISM – Socialist governments want more regulation and control over the state's money. Socialism tries to distribute wealth, by offering financial help to the poor and taxing the rich.

LIBERALISM – Liberals believe the government should help the citizen to help themselves. Their view on capitalism is to regulate where it's needed, and allow each citizen the freedom to make money.

CONSERVATISM – Conservatism promotes private ownership and conserving what people have. This matches the idea of capitalism and the free market. Conservatives favour less regulation and more economic freedom.

SHARE *and* SHARE ALIKE

On the EXTREME LEFT of the *ideas rainbow* sits a political movement called COMMUNISM. It believes that everything should be SHARED OUT EQUALLY TO EVERYONE. It is considered to be the OPPOSITE OF CAPITALISM.

> "Let the ruling classes tremble at a communist revolution. The proletarians have nothing to lose but their chains. They have a world to win. Workingmen of all countries, unite!"

Karl Marx (1818–1883) was a German philosopher and social scientist who studied the effect of capitalism on society. From his research and his political involvement, Marx created ideas that became the foundation of modern communism.

THE BOSS vs THE WORKERS

Marx identified a class system in the capitalist system of his day. At the top of the class tree was the boss of the company, who got wealthier as the company made lots of profit. At the bottom were the employees who made very little money for all their hard work. Marx called the wealthy elite "the bourgeoisie", and the workers he called "the proletariat". Marxism was about bridging the gap between the two and distributing wealth more evenly throughout society.

REVOLUTION!

Marx's solution to this class imbalance was a two-stage revolution. First the proletariat would rise and overthrow the ruling bourgeoisie. This should be easy because there were more proletariat than bourgeoisie. Second, after a period of dictatorship by the "many poor" over the "few rich", the two classes would sort out their differences and become equal. This would then lead to a state that would distribute everything equally. If you needed food for your family you were given enough to eat. Marx believed everyone would then work hard for the state.

58

PROS AND CONS

After a period of political influence, the past 25 years has seen communism slowly lose its grip on world politics. But where did communism go wrong? Well, it didn't quite work out as Marx had hoped. Instead of the revolution leading to a state of equality, the only way to keep control was to use autocratic techniques. The strict regimes led to unrest and further revolutions, turning the states back to capitalism. But communism wasn't a complete failure, it has contributed greatly to science, with the first artificial satellite, first man, and first woman in space all achieved by the then communist USSR (now Russia).

GOOD BAD

WHAT IS COMMUNISM?

COMMUNISM is a way of dealing with the *money in society*. It takes an opposite approach to CAPITALISM, so instead of everyone seeking profit to better themselves, everything, including money, is DISTRIBUTED equally.

shops

farms

factories

FREE

PROPERTY

THE MEANS OF PRODUCTION

Marx believed it was important for the state to own all of what he called the MEANS OF PRODUCTION, which included all the factories, farms, and shops. This meant that all the profits would go to the state, not the greedy bosses, and would then be invested back into the state and its citizens. This was the opposite view to capitalism, which promoted private ownership and personal wealth.

REVOLT FOR FREE CARD

In 1917, Vladimir Lenin masterminded a revolution in the name of communism and overthrew the Russian monarchy. He believed the proletariat were incapable of overthrowing capitalism by themselves, so decided to form a party to fight for the proletariat's interests.

Vladimir Lenin (1870–1924)

This is the NEWS

CONTROL

All governments have information that the citizen doesn't have access to. Some information is important to pass on, but some could create unrest or panic. For this reason governments control what information leaves the halls of power.

CENSORSHIP

One way to control the flow of information is to censor it. This means the citizen is informed of certain facts, but the sensitive pieces of information are left out. Governments write press releases saying exactly what they want the news agencies to know.

PROPAGANDA

Propaganda is an extreme version of censorship. Instead of releasing facts about what is happening inside government, the people in power create a false truth by exaggerating pieces of information. Propaganda was used a lot during the Second World War to keep up the citizens' morale.

News keeps the *citizens* up to speed with what is happening in the state, and elsewhere in the world. It also gives the government the chance to communicate with the citizens.

INFORMATION

GO

TV

News channels and programmes report on current affairs. 24-hour news channels can broadcast live events and breaking stories. In some countries, the government can control the channel's content.

ONLINE

Dedicated Internet sites and forums also report news. The Internet is hard to control, but in some states the government can block its citizens from accessing certain sites.

NOT THE NEWS – HOW BORING! Believe it or not the news you read, hear, or watch plays an important role in politics. The MEDIA (newspapers, TV, radio, internet, and even films and books) keep us updated with what's happening in the political world. In the modern world information is power!

DIVERSION

TOP SECRET

A government tries to keep its citizens safe and happy. Sometimes this means keeping secrets. All states have secrets they don't want other states and sometimes even their own citizens to know. Why so secretive? A government will have access to sensitive information on the strength of its military, wealth of the state, and any weaknesses. It doesn't want this type of information to fall into the wrong hands.

PUBLIC OPINION

With the growth of democracy, what the citizen thinks has gained power in politics. Without public opinion on its side, a government will struggle to keep power. Politicians test speeches and use special surveys, called polls, to find out what citizens want. Citizens also hold politicians to account – if they don't perform the citizens can vote for someone else.

LEAKS!

From time to time the tight-lipped government may get a leak. Information it wants to control can seep out and become public knowledge. A rogue politician or government employee may open his or her mouth, data may be hacked, or documents may be left on the train. Governments have to deal with these situations and try to control any damage they cause. But is it best for the public to know?

NEWSPAPER

These are printed daily or weekly to keep the citizens up-to-date with current affairs. Some newspapers give their support to a political party or individual.

Local POLITICS

Politics doesn't just happen in one big, impressive-looking building. It is all around you. At the heart of politics are *local issues* that all add up into what are then considered to be NATIONAL PROBLEMS.

JIGSAW POLITICS

A government has to keep its citizens happy. This means solving problems that they think are important. Local issues and needs can lead to bigger decisions that can help the state as a whole.

THE PIECES OF A JIGSAW
Several local issues can all add up into a problem that the state government needs to deal with.

1. **Local corner shops** are losing business to a big supermarket.

2. **Local fishermen** are being forced out of business by a bigger rival.

3. A town has **lost its main industry** and people are leaving.

4. **Unemployment** figures are high in rural towns.

5. **Fewer jobs** are available for local university leavers.

Local PEOPLE

Local government looks to help the local citizens of a specific region and carries their concerns forward to the national level. Local politicians are voted in by the local residents and they look to solve the problems that arise in cities, towns, and villages. Local governments also appoint leaders who help guide and control the local agenda.

POLITICS AT HOME

Have a look around your home and neighbourhood. You will see services and items that are dealt with by the government. The ideas for these services were worked out in national government, but the local services are carried out and maintained by local politicians and councils.

RUBBISH COLLECTION
Local councils decide what days rubbish is collected and how much can be recycled or put into landfill.

WATER SERVICES
Local companies can supply and maintain the local water supply to your home.

ROAD MAINTENANCE
The local council will fund improvements and repairs to the roads near your home.

EMERGENCIES
Local police, ambulance, fire, and coastguard stations react to emergencies in your area.

THE BIGGER PICTURE
Some local governments are allowed to handle certain problems. But some local issues are taken to the national government, which has more resources to help. In the case of our jigsaw they may decide to help local businesses with grants of money or tax relief. This will help create new jobs and companies in the areas that need them.

Don't SHOOT the messenger

Here's a quick history of diplomacy.

1 At the very beginning, thousands of years ago, if a stranger strayed onto someone else's territory, the locals would protect their land and attack the stranger.

2 After several years, neighbouring states realized they could achieve more by not shooting the messenger. This became the ancient principle of diplomacy. Messengers were soon seen as "mouth-pieces" of the ruler.

3 Soon the messenger's role became very important to foreign relations and they became known as AMBASSADORS. An ambassador's main role was to serve his or her home state's interests in foreign lands.

> A stranger to our lands! SHOOT HIM!

THE MESSENGER

> DON'T shoot the messenger!

> Okay.

> Ambassador, you are really spoiling us!

MODERN DIPLOMACY

Today, diplomacy is the most important way to deal with foreign relations. Ambassadors are now known as diplomats, but they are no longer alone on the diplomatic road for resolution.

Summits
These are where groups of leaders or diplomats get together for a common cause. Summits are held to stop wars or solve global issues, like the environment.

Unofficial diplomacy
This is when a famous person, such as a film star, goes to a country to help highlight and publicize issues.

Actress Angelina Jolie on a diplomatic mission

Special envoys
This is when a neutral representative goes to help states that are fighting. Special envoys have helped broker peace deals in Northern Ireland and have progressed the Middle East peace process.

Imagine living in a world without mobile phones, aeroplanes, or the Internet. Communication with other states would be really hard – but it's also really important because it can stop states from arguing and going to war.

It all began many, many years ago...

4 With more ambassadors crisscrossing the world they needed official residences in foreign countries, and so the EMBASSY BUILDING was created.

> As safe as home...

THE EMBASSY

Cardinal de Richelieu (1585–1642)

Centralized embassies

The art of diplomacy took a huge organized step forward in France during the 17th century. The country's First Minister, Cardinal de Richelieu, organized the embassies so he could control the information coming into and leaving France.

5 Unfortunately, having ambassadors and embassies didn't stop wars. After a lot of conflicts, neighbouring states realized it was best to try a little harder to get on. Diplomacy became the first choice in settling arguments and this led to the diplomatic unions and summits that are commonplace today.

> Let's have a chat and see what we can do.

food medicine clothes

Concert of Europe

At the Congress of Vienna in 1814, warring nations in Europe decided to put their differences behind them and agreed on a regular meeting where ambassadors would get together and discuss problems. This was known as the Concert of Europe and was the start of the idea of the European Union. Unfortunately, it didn't last long and more wars broke out.

HOME AWAY FROM HOME

When on holiday, you might lose your passport or find yourself in trouble. Your state's embassy should be your first port of call because they can help deal with your problems.

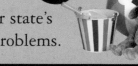

Chance

THIS CARD MAY BE KEPT UNTIL NEEDED, OR SOLD

GET OUT OF JAIL FREE

Immunity

In most countries DIPLOMATS are immune from the laws of the state they are stationed in. This rule has been customary for many years, and was officially legalized by the Vienna Convention in 1961.

I spy with my little eye...

The diplomat's role on foreign soil gives them access to important information and buildings. Over the years there have been many allegations of diplomats spying on state secrets.

Working

Politics can cross borders. Neighbouring countries help each other out, join forces, or have disagreements. Wars, natural disasters, and crises affect everyone no matter where you live. So to help out, states banded together to create the United Nations.

UNITED NATIONS

When was it created?
On 24th October 1945, the 51 founding countries set up the United Nations.

Why?
World War II had just ended and the UN was created to make sure a third world war would never happen.

Who?
The initial charter was drawn up by representatives from China, the Soviet Union, the UK, and the USA. The name United Nations was coined by US president Franklin Roosevelt.

How does it function?
The UN has a unique charter that allows it to take action on a variety of social, economic, and military issues. It also creates a forum for its member states to raise problems or offer help and solutions.

Above: The UN logo

Left: The UN's headquarters, based in New York.

IT IS MADE UP OF:

1 General Assembly
All member states are represented by a delegation of five people who sit in the General Assembly. This is the main part of the UN and is where all the big decisions are made. When voting, each member state is equal – they all get one vote.

WE VOTE

TOGETHER

2 Security Council
This is a smaller council of 15 members, of which five are permanent members (these are the USA, Russia, China, France and the UK). The remaining 10 members are selected by the General Assembly on a rotation system. The council has special powers and generally acts on major issues affecting war and peace. They work out how best to resolve conflicts and can impose sanctions on guilty states.

Countries working together

Switzerland was an observer state from 1948 until it joined the UN on 10th September 2002.

MAP KEY: At the moment the UN consists of 193 member states. The UN looks to maintain peace and security around the world, help countries develop and deal with social and economic problems, and protects human rights.

together

What is a coalition?

A coalition is when two or more countries join together for a common purpose. Political parties may form a coalition in government, and states can form global unions.

3 Economic and Social Council

This council deals with the world's monetary, social, and environmental problems. It tries to improve living standards and education by promoting trade and economic cooperation.

4 International Court of Justice

The Court of Justice is the only main part of the UN that isn't based in New York. It sits in The Hague in the Netherlands and rules on international disputes and other issues referred to it by member states. The council is made up of 15 elected judges who serve for nine years.

as UNITED NATIONS

Republic of South Sudan was the last to join the UN on 14th July 2011.

The only non-member, observer states are Vatican City and Palestine.

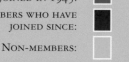

ORIGINAL MEMBERS WHO JOINED IN 1945:	
MEMBERS WHO HAVE JOINED SINCE:	
NON-MEMBERS:	

5 Secretariat

These are the employees of the UN. They work under the Secretary General, who is treated as a head of state. They deal with the day-to-day aspects from each different department. In 2013, there were 44,000 UN employees.

OTHER COALITIONS

The European Union

Europe has tried on many occasions to create coalitions – formal and informal. In 1951 six countries, France, Belgium, Italy, Luxembourg, Germany, and the Netherlands, created the European Coal and Steel Community. In 1993, after several changes, this became the European Union.

ASEAN

The Association of South East Asian Nations (ASEAN) is currently only an economic and political grouping of smaller South East Asian countries (excluding China, Japan, and India).

MERCOSUR

MERCOSUR in South America includes Argentina, Brazil, Uruguay, Paraguay, and Venezuela. It promotes trade and economic growth within the region.

NATO

The North Atlantic Treaty Organization (NATO) is a military alliance that cooperates in military and peace-keeping missions. It has 28 member states from North America and Europe.

All the above regional coalitions have to follow the principles of the United Nations.

These are the logos of some of the many coalitions in the world.

When STATES *don't* get along

In politics not everyone agrees. This is also the case when it comes to international relations. When diplomacy and talking fails there are several other ways to end a disagreement.

IT'S GOOD TO TALK!

Since the creation of the United Nations in 1945, states have agreed to live together peacefully and to resolve disputes through negotiations or arbitration. The International Court of Justice is always ready to hear disputes and to suggest solutions, provided the countries involved will let them.

MAIN METHODS OF DEALING WITH TROUBLESOME STATES

TRADE SANCTIONS To change the behaviour of a troublesome state, other countries that trade with it can restrict the import and export of goods. These sanctions start with weapons and then spread to other areas of the economy, including food and fuel.

STOP AID Some states need help from others to function. So an offending state may have its aid (technology, education, food, or money) restricted until it stops its bad behaviour.

EXCLUDING BAD STATES Another non-violent way to stop a disagreement is to exclude the guilty state from certain activities.

BOYCOTTING Other states can "boycott" the troublesome state, which means stopping certain activities. They may stop buying products or playing sport with the guilty state, or stop them participating in international cultural events.

INTERNATIONAL COALITIONS The guilty state may lose powers within a coalition or international group, like the UNITED NATIONS. This will force them to make changes to their policies or force them to make peace.

THREATS OF FORCE If all else fails then the arguing state or states may have to be threatened with force. This is one of the last ports of call when dealing with disagreements, and usually involves the UN Security Council, which passes a resolution to authorize other countries to use military action.

ARMS RACES It was once thought that stockpiling weapons was the best way to keep peace and deter others from becoming threatening. But it just led to very tense, near-war scenarios.

What is a *superpower?*

WHAT'S TO DISAGREE ABOUT?

The first thing that causes disagreements is when states want to stretch their borders and get their hands on more land, which belongs to another state. Fortunately no one owns the sea, though states can exercise control over the coastline up to 19 km (12 miles) out, and can exercise economic control for up to 320 km (200 miles).

WAR (WHAT IS IT GOOD FOR?)

Wars have occurred throughout history, many of which have been savage and have resulted in widespread destruction. Most of the conflicts have been local or regional, but we have also suffered two WORLD WARS, as well as other international conflicts that have killed millions of people. This is why war should be the last resort of any disagreement.

WHY GO TO WAR?

War is only used when it is the only option to stop an argument or remove a threat. At present the UN system only allows a country to go to war if it is attacked. This is meant to stop arms races, rivalries, and other forms of confrontation.

A superpower is a state that is seen as very powerful in the eyes of other states. The USA is considered to be the current top superpower and is very influential around the world.

"To jaw-jaw is *always better* than to WAR-WAR."

Sir Winston Churchill, former British Prime Minister.

PEOPLE *and* politics

Can we, the citizens, have a say about how our states are run? What power to influence politics do we all have?

In many states, mostly democracies, citizens have been given rights and freedoms, such as the right to vote and the freedom of speech. These give citizens the opportunity to voice their opinions, choose governments to lead them, and demonstrate against unpopular political decisions.

Citizens in a democracy have the power to make or break a government, which forces those in politics to listen to "the people".

It's up to each one of us to decide whether we do nothing or use our rights to shape the politics of our states.

I can make a *difference!*

What *is a* constitution?

Many countries have a written (or unwritten) set of laws that set out how the state should be governed. This is called a constitution. Constitutions divide responsibility between different parts of the government so no one person, or group of people, has all the power, and allow citizens to be involved in the decision-making. Within a constitution, there are **three main parts.**

We think of the ideas for the government's policies.

A CONSTITUTION

DEFINES THE ROLE OF GOVERNMENT

THE EXECUTIVE
The Executive is responsible for making government policies and carrying them out. These policies get passed onto the Legislature...

DEFINES THE SYSTEM OF GOVERNMENT

UNITARY SYSTEM
A central government is responsible for making policies for the whole state. They may instruct several local government authorities to carry them out.

OR

OUTLINES THE RIGHTS OF CITIZENS

POLITICAL RIGHTS
Legal and moral rights vary from state to state but may include right to vote, freedom of speech, and right to education.

AND

"ONE COUNTRY, ONE CONSTITUTION,

FAMOUS CONSTITUTIONS

 US constitution This was first written in the late-18th century as a result of a revolution removing the authority of the British government and replacing it with a United States Congress.

 European constitution During 2004, a constitution document was created to involve all members of the European Union, but this was never agreed. It was replaced by the Lisbon Treaty in 2009.

 Indian constitution India has the longest written constitution in the world with 444 articles, or sections. It took almost three years of discussion to compile the document.

On 17th September 1787, the US constitution was signed in Philadelphia by 42 delegates, including George Washington who became the first president.

All looks ok to us.

Now we're going to make sure that everyone sticks to the rules!

THE LEGISLATURE
The Legislature is responsible for examining and approving the Executive's policies before they can be carried out.

THE JUDICIARY
The Judiciary is responsible for deciding if the laws of the state have been followed or not.

FEDERAL SYSTEM
A federal system is when a state is divided into regions and has two levels of government: a national one making policies for the whole state, and a regional government level.

CONFEDERAL SYSTEM
In a confederate, the regional government level that makes the laws on internal affairs also tells the state government what to do.

HUMAN RIGHTS
Basic rights and freedoms that all people should receive for their survival and their dignity. Some states recognize more than others.

Human rights include those that are against the actions of the state, such as the right not to be arrested without cause, the right to equality before the law, and property rights.

Amnesty International campaigns for human rights around the world. This is their logo. It symbolizes the light of hope.

Rights and responsibilities

GETTING THE BALANCE RIGHT

IN THE CLASSROOM

You might wonder why being able to go to school is a right you want. Education gives us lifelong skills, without which lives cannot be improved. It helps children get out of poverty and stay healthy, but it is a right denied to millions around the world who can't get to school or are unable to concentrate in class.

> We have the RESPONSIBILITY not to stop others from learning.

> Can I have my book back please!

Millions of children have to work and are denied an education.

IN THE STREET

Living in a safe, sustainable, and clean environment is considered a basic human right as everyone deserves to be happy, healthy, and protected.

> We have the RIGHT to enjoy a healthy environment.

> We have the RIGHT to an education.

Caring for our environment, recycling, and using sustainable resources are all part of the responsibility of making lives better for ourselves, others, and future generations.

Each day, 14,000 people die from unclean water.

unicef

The *United Nations Children's Fund* supports the Convention on the Rights of the Child (1989).

In many countries, the political and human rights of a citizen are outlined as part of a state's constitution, which the government should follow. The number and type of rights varies from state to state. Along with having these rights, being a citizen also involves a legal and moral responsibility to obey laws and do the correct thing so others can receive their rights, too.

IN THE WORLD

The right to equality and freedom from discrimination are the top two articles, or items, of the Universal Declaration of Human Rights (1948). Respecting others and having own self-respect and dignity was considered the key to peace amongst all members of the human family.

We have the RESPONSIBILITY not to drop litter or make the environment unpleasant for others.

We all have a RIGHT to be treated equally.

We have the RESPONSIBILITY not to hurt others or set them apart.

HUMAN RIGHTS IN ACTION

In 1948, a few years after World War II, the United Nations, an international organization of countries, produced the Universal Declaration of Human Rights. This list of 30 articles covered the rights and freedoms that everybody should have with the aim to bring freedom, peace, and justice in the world.

CONFLICTING RIGHTS

Sometimes situations can occur when two rights conflict, for example, a film star's right to personal privacy and a newspaper's right to freedom of speech. These cases are taken to the law courts for the judiciary to decide which right should take priority.

I say, no photos please. This is a private wedding.

Each child has the right to education, health care, food, shelter, play, protection, and much more.

The right *to vote*

In a democracy, the right to vote is the main way most citizens can influence the decisions about how their country is governed. Citizens get their chance when the government decides to hold an election. An election is when the citizens who can vote are given the chance to choose their political leader or government representative.

RUNNING AN ELECTION CAMPAIGN

To win an election, politicians have to persuade people to support them. Each political party needs to identify their policies (plan of action), explaining what they would do if they were elected.

1 Write a manifesto
Each political party prepares a list of actions, or policies, that the party promises to carry out if they are elected. This is called a manifesto.

We promise to...

2 Meet the voters
The candidates (representatives from each party) travel about meeting people in their area to explain their ideas and convince the voters to choose them.

3 Publicize the manifesto
Political parties try to persuade citizens to vote for them by distributing leaflets and posters, and promoting their ideas and personality on television and radio.

4 Encourage active voting
On the day of the election, the politicians encourage people to go to the polling station to vote.

POLLING STATION

Would you like a lift to the polling station?

"THE BALLOT IS STRONGER THAN

WHO IS ALLOWED TO VOTE?

> In 1893, New Zealand was the first country to give women the right to vote. Since then most other countries do too, although often after much campaigning by groups of women known as suffragettes.

Governments make laws to say who can vote and this differs between countries. Most demand that the voter must be a citizen of the country and have reached a certain age – 18 years in most countries. Some governments prevent certain people from voting, such as prisoners and women. In Australia, the law states that everyone has to vote – those who do not are fined.

ELECTRONIC VOTING IN INDIA

The mark to use on a ballot paper varies in different countries, such as with a cross, a tick, or a thumbprint. In India, citizens vote by pressing their preference on an electronic device inside the booths.

Have you taken part in a vote? Perhaps it was to choose a classmate to become a school council representative. How did you decide who to vote for?

AT THE BALLOT BOOTH

Citizens make their choice in secret by marking a ballot paper and putting this into a ballot box that is not opened until after the polls (casting of votes) have closed. Depending on the type of voting system used, the ballot paper has to be marked in a certain way.

FIRST PAST THE POST

The citizen makes a mark on the ballot paper next to the candidate they support. The candidate with the most votes wins.

SUPPLEMENTARY VOTE

The ballot paper has two columns. The citizen marks their first choice candidate in the first column and, if they wish, a second choice candidate in the second column. If the first choice candidate gets more than 50% then they win, if not the second preferences of the two highest candidates are counted and the winner is the one with most votes.

ALTERNATIVE VOTE

The citizen numbers the candidates in order of preference on the ballot paper. If no candidate has a majority of first preferences, then the one with the least votes is ruled out and then second preferences are counted. This continues until one candidate has a clear majority.

Booths are set up so each voter can mark the ballot paper in secret.

Name	
Mr Jones	
Mrs Singh	
Ms Patti	✕
Mr Rama	
Mr Smith	
Mr Costa	
Mrs Jacobs	
Ms Smart	

The ballot paper above uses the "first past the post" voting system.

Name	1st	2nd
Mr Jones		
Mrs Singh		
Ms Patti	✕	
Mr Rama		
Mr Smith		
Mr Costa		✕
Mrs Jacobs		
Ms Smart		

The ballot paper above uses the "supplementary" voting system.

Name	Order 1-8
Mr Jones	8
Mrs Singh	4
Ms Patti	1
Mr Rama	7
Mr Smith	5
Mr Costa	2
Mrs Jacobs	3
Ms Smart	6

The ballot paper above uses the "alternative" voting system.

THE BULLET." Abraham Lincoln (1809–1865)

A *difference* of opinion

How does a citizen decide whom to *vote* for? Ideally, voters need to be well informed about the *different* ideas of each political party so that they can form an *opinion*. Differences of opinion are healthy for politics and through *debate* opposing viewpoints can be discussed.

How a debate works...

A statement, or motion, is made that can be agreed or disagreed with.

Good preparation is everything...
The debaters research information about the issue and form their arguments to either agree or disagree with the motion.

The debate begins
The debaters present their arguments to persuade others to agree with them. Both sides should respect each other.

> NOW I'VE DONE MY RESEARCH ...

> I PROPOSE THAT...

> I REJECT YOUR PROPOSAL BECAUSE...

Then the voters decide
The listeners can form their opinion about which debater to support. A vote may be taken to find out which idea was the most popular.

People who find that they share influences their thinking on other

THE RIGHT TO FREEDOM OF SPEECH

Being able to speak out to share ideas and opinions with others is recognized as an international human right. Through debating ideas and voicing differences of opinion, laws can be made and changed.

The right to freedom of speech allows citizens to protest, such as these Australian aboriginal children are doing.

What's your opinion?

Think about the argument for and against each of these motions:

MOTION 1.
Recycling should become a law.

MOTION 2.
Keeping animals as pets should be banned.

MOTION 3.
Everyone should be required to carry identity cards.

For example, you could argue *against* the motion by saying...
• pets provide companionship.
• owning a pet teaches someone responsibility and caring.

Or *for* the motion by saying...
• that animals should live in the wild.
• that pets in a house are unhygienic because they carry pests and diseases.

THE BIG ISSUE

Your opinion in one subject can influence your views in other subjects. For example, do you worry about the environment and the survival of the planet? If so, does this effect what you think about air travel, mining, deforestation (cutting down forests), and vegetarianism?

Should I use plastic bags?

What do you think about deforestation?

Should air travel be restricted?

What do you think about mining?

Is vegetarianism a good thing?

common views on the BIG issues, which then issues, may join together and form political parties.

FREEDOM OF EXPRESSION

The right to form associations

Under PRESSURE

Another way citizens can try to influence governments is to become part of a pressure group or interest group. People who share a common interest join together to persuade people in power to support their views.

CHANGE! IMPROVE! STOP!

MAKING AN IMPACT

These are some of the features of pressure groups that make governments listen to them:

Strength in numbers

The larger the group the more impact citizens are able to make, such as by holding protests and demonstrations, disrupting parts of the country.

Protesters demonstrate against the G20 Summit in Pittsburgh, Pennsylvania, USA.

Economic pulling-power

Trade unions are associations of workers interested in protecting their working conditions and wages. If discontented, they may strike, closing down the workplace.

Striking workers protest in Cape Town, South Africa.

Media interest

Groups whose causes are highlighted by the media may then receive huge support from the voting public.

British actress Joanna Lumley got media interest in the Gurkhas' cause.

Financial resources

Groups who have plenty of money from supporters can produce publicity material known as propaganda, and even hire full-time workers.

Greenpeace can afford a boat.

Access to information

Governments request information from some groups to make political decisions. These groups can use the passing on of the information to their advantage.

Governments decide farming subsidies based on the information provided by farming unions.

Children from many countries were involved in the events held during the UN Special Session on Children. Some children were invited to speak to the UN General Assembly, such as these children from Uganda.

> "A man will fight harder for his interests than for his rights."
>
> Napoleon Bonaparte (1769–1821)

MORE!

MAKING DECISIONS

Good... Between elections, pressure groups are a way of forcing governments to listen to public opinion. Their views also provide the government with an all-round picture on which to decide policies.

... or bad?

However, if discussions between lobbyists (pressure group members) and government representatives are carried out in private, leading to decisions being made in secret, then this would be undemocratic and may lead to corruption. Larger and wealthier pressure groups could also have more influence on the government than the smaller and lesser-known ones, whose interests might oppose them.

UN Special Session on Children
In 2002, the United Nations (UN) General Assembly held an event aiming to commit nations to a set of goals for improving lives of young people around the world.

HOW TO APPLY PRESSURE

1 Lobby a politician
A group meets a government minister or administrator who is responsible for the group's area of interest, to gain political support.

2 Promises of support
A group encourages a government representative to represent their interests by promising that their members will vote for him or her and by providing campaign funds.

3 Hold a demonstration
A group promotes their interest through the media and by demonstrating to gain public support.

4 Go to court
A group takes their issue to the courts to change the interpretation of the laws in favour of their interest.

5 Use a celebrity
A group finds a film star or well-known or prominent person who supports their interest, and can be a figurehead for the campaign.

American actor George Clooney speaks during the "Save Darfur Now" rally in Washington DC, USA, in 2006.

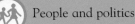

FUNDING *and*

A citizen's voting decision can be influenced by how a political party intends to **run the *economy*** and **spend taxes**. A country's economy describes the *exchange of money, goods, or services* within that

How an economy works:

BUSINESSES provide jobs, goods, and services for the people. Out of the income (profits) made from what they sell, they pay taxes to the government.

Businesses

Health care

Transport

SCHOOL

Housing

PUBLIC SERVICES

TAXES

SHARE certificate

DHL

MONEY, INVESTMENTS

WAGES

WORK, LABOUR

GOODS AND SERVICES

The government, businesses, and citizens rely on each other in the economy chain.

CRASH!

If just one of these links in the chain collapses then the economy can crash. For example, many businesses rely on investors to loan them money. If investors stop loaning money, then businesses can't hire people, so make and sell fewer goods and services, and so pay less tax to the government. As the chain collapses, people lose jobs and have less to spend, businesses fail, and governments cannot provide public services.

Citizens

LESS MONEY FOR PUBLIC SERVICES
FEWER TAXES

NO MONEY
LOWER WAGES
FEWER JOBS
FEWER GOODS, SERVICES

MORE TAXES
FEWER PUBLIC SERVICES
FEWER JOBS

Out of their income (wages), CITIZENS pay taxes to the government and with the remaining money pay for services and choose what goods to buy and what amount to invest in businesses.

FINANCE

country and the management of these resources. There is a *balance* between how involved the government is in this process, and the amount of freedom given to businesses and to citizens to make their own *financial choices*.

With their income (money from taxes), the GOVERNMENT has to make sure that people are educated, housed, feel safe, kept healthy, and can get to work, so that businesses can also run smoothly.

Government

Police

TAXES

PUBLIC SERVICES

WORK, LABOUR

GANDHI'S IDEAL

The Indian spiritual and political leader Mahatma Gandhi (1869–1948) believed that an individual's well-being was more important than economic profits for industrialists. He encouraged thousands of villagers to earn a living by making their own clothing, crafts, and tools so that they would work hard for their own profit. This stopped India's reliance on foreign goods and businesses, which was causing poverty and oppression.

His two economic principles:

Principle 1: If a nation has a high population then machines should not be used so that all people can have work and earn a wage.
Principle 2: A nation should only produce as much as it needs. Extra production leads to an international economic race, which leads to exploitation (low wages) of the people.

PRINCIPLES

Rights and regulations

Simply, economies can be divided into two types: a **free market** economy and a **planned** economy. In a **free market economy**, people and businesses can make their own decisions based on supply and demand, which makes prices rise and fall. The government just sets out a few regulations to make sure that businesses are not misinforming or charging unfairly. Consumers can buy what they want when they want and businesses can compete for profit.

Price rises

Demand falls
Supply rises

Demand rises
Supply falls

Price falls

In a **planned economy**, the government has control over all parts of the economy, fixing prices and wages. Services are free as these are paid for through taxes.

Inflation

For both economies, if governments don't have enough money to cover all their costs, then they are forced to print more money, which leads to the inflation of the state's currency, lowering its value.

83

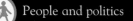

How to stage a *coup d'etat?*

Coup d'etat is French for "stroke of the state" and means a **sudden overthrow** of a state's government. Rather than waiting for an *election* to change a weak government, a small group, often led by military officers, take control by FORCE. A *new government* might be established, which may or may not be democratic, or the situation could lead to a REVOLUTION, when the political system is completely changed.

On the day of the coup d'etat...   At the same time...

The group storms the government buildings.   The group takes over all ways of communication...

A short while later...   A little later...

The government is unable to resist.   Emergency measures are put in place for running the state.

The government is weak...

Here's how it's done:

THE CABINET

The citizens are unhappy about the way the state is run.

A small group meet in secret.

The group plans to overthrow the government.

CASHIER

... and the transport network... *... and the state's power supplies...* *... and takes control of state finances.*

A month or two later...

Order is restored to the state.

What happens now?

THE CABINET

The coup leaders decide how the state will be governed.

Government of the *future*...

The politics of our world are forever *changing* and having to ADAPT to technological advancements, environmental issues, and events that affect many nations. The *role* of governments and citizens' INVOLVEMENT

IS A GLOBAL GOVERNMENT NEEDED?

At present, state governments deal with national issues and a handful of international organizations, such as the United Nations and the International Monetary Fund, deal with issues that affect many nations. However, there are increasingly more global issues that governments around the world have to deal with and collaborate on.

The United Nations system, set up in 1945, has helped to encourage collaboration between governments, but it has not succeeded in stopping all wars and disputes and has been unable to get all countries committed to international treaties, such as the Kyoto Protocol on climate change.

Some states view themselves as more powerful than others and nationalism – pride in the strength of their own country – means that a single global government where all states are equal and no boundaries between countries exist may never happen.

> How would global government representatives be elected?

> Would state governments be willing to give up power over national policies?

Would a single global government be best to deal with the challenges of the future?

AN ALTERNATIVE...

Imagine citizen-led politics

Could citizens decide the policies? In this technological age, the Internet has become a space for citizens around the world to freely express their ideas, access information, and participate in politics.

Imagine a nationless world

In 1971, John Lennon wrote a song called *Imagine*, which described a world where there were no countries so no causes for conflicts and all resources such as food were shared. In this imagined world, people would view themselves as citizens of the world.

"I hope someday you'll join us... And the

AND BEYOND

in politics is always open to **debate** and *discussion*. So what will governments be like in the *FUTURE,* and will the idea of just *one global government* ever work?

IMAGINE A UNIVERSAL GOVERNMENT

In the far-distant future, we may discover that humans are just one species of a universe of citizens. It's the imaginings of many science-fiction films, novels, and Internet sites. Would a universal government be needed to maintain equality, peace, justice, and cooperation between citizens from different planets?

Who will be the overall leader? Who decides?

Will citizens from one planet have the same rights on other planets?

Will freedoms be given to all races and species?

What laws should there be for space travel between planets?

How would a universal government be set up – a unitary system with a central universal government or a federation with separate planet governments, or will we think of something completely new?

YOU DECIDE

What do you think should be in a universal constitution, be the rights of the universal citizens, and be the answer to universal political issues?

Universal constitution

Who's in charge? Will there be an Executive, a Legislature, and a Judiciary or some new group to divide up the responsibility, prevent bad decisions, and enforce the laws?

Universal rights

Will rights and freedoms be given to all races and species? Should rights be given to all animals, even a housefly? Do citizens have the right to move freely in and out of different planets? Will all citizens have the rights to the same resources, such as water shared around all planets?

Universal policies

Is each planet responsible for maintaining its own transport, education, health care systems etc. or should it be the universal government so that standards are the same on every planet? Will there be a universal currency, or one or more currencies on each planet?

world will live as one." *Imagine,* John Lennon

GETTING INTO POLITICS

Try this *quiz* to find out how YOU could get **involved** in politics...

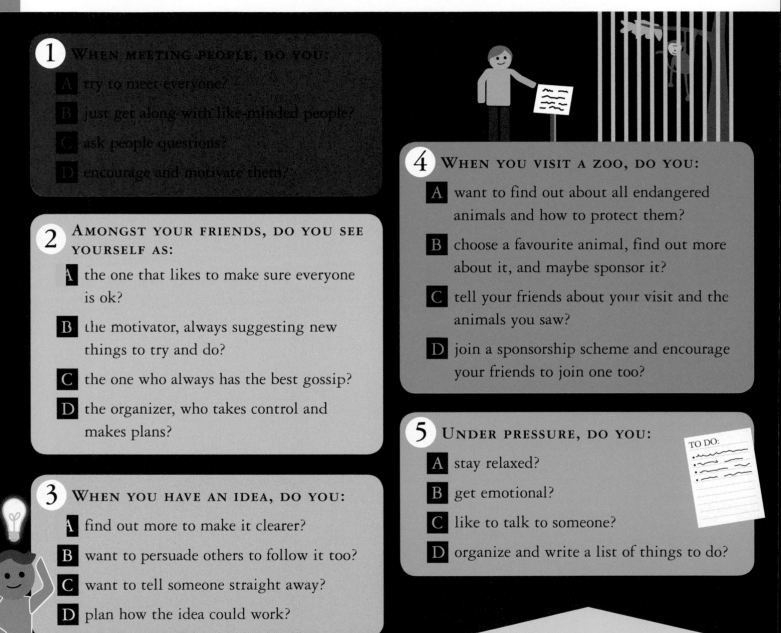

1 WHEN MEETING PEOPLE, DO YOU:

A try to meet everyone?

B just get along with like-minded people?

C ask people questions?

D encourage and motivate them?

2 AMONGST YOUR FRIENDS, DO YOU SEE YOURSELF AS:

A the one that likes to make sure everyone is ok?

B the motivator, always suggesting new things to try and do?

C the one who always has the best gossip?

D the organizer, who takes control and makes plans?

3 WHEN YOU HAVE AN IDEA, DO YOU:

A find out more to make it clearer?

B want to persuade others to follow it too?

C want to tell someone straight away?

D plan how the idea could work?

4 WHEN YOU VISIT A ZOO, DO YOU:

A want to find out about all endangered animals and how to protect them?

B choose a favourite animal, find out more about it, and maybe sponsor it?

C tell your friends about your visit and the animals you saw?

D join a sponsorship scheme and encourage your friends to join one too?

5 UNDER PRESSURE, DO YOU:

A stay relaxed?

B get emotional?

C like to talk to someone?

D organize and write a list of things to do?

TO DO:

RESULTS

More playground equipment!

MOSTLY As: *You have the skills to become a government representative.* To work as a member of parliament will require a strong passion for politics, the ability to cope well under pressure, and confidence to speak to many different people. Get some experience now by joining your school's debating society or school council to get your opinions heard.

MOSTLY Bs: *You have the skills to become a member of a pressure group.* Pressure group members belong to organizations that believe in a cause with the aim of influencing political decisions. If there is something you feel very strongly about, for example fairness in the playground, why not try to start up your own group and persuade other people to join you?

Now you've learnt so much about the *fascinating* world of politics, it may be worth considering a future **career** as a government representative or a political reporter... Start now and let your ambition take you FAR!

6 WHEN YOU RECYCLE RUBBISH, DO YOU:

A think about the environment and other ways you could help?

B encourage others to recycle as much as possible?

C find out if your friends recycle too and what else they do to help the environment?

D encourage your friends to recycle, save energy, share lifts, and save water?

7 WHEN YOU SHOP, DO YOU:

A read the labels of where every item was made and think about the people who produced them?

B show your friends what you bought and encourage them to buy the same?

C find out where your friends shop and go there too?

D encourage friends to buy things that are made locally?

8 WHEN IT COMES TO SOCIAL NETWORK SITES, DO YOU:

A mainly use them to keep up with what's going on in your friends' lives and what is making them happy or sad?

B prefer to create groups about specific things and then encourage your friends to join?

C sign up to every networking site and make regular updates and blogs about your thoughts?

D use them mostly to arrange events and invite as many people as possible?

9 WHEN YOU HAVE AN OPINION, DO YOU:

A debate it with other people?

B persuade others to share your viewpoint?

C write it down and let others read it?

D find others who share your viewpoint and encourage them to tell others?

MOSTLY Cs: *You have the skills to become a political reporter.* The media is very influential in politics. The public can be swayed greatly by what they read in newspapers and see on news reports. A political reporter follows current affairs and is able to write stories about the government in an informative and impartial manner. You could start now by writing an article for your school's newsletter.

MOSTLY Ds: *You have the skills to become a campaign manager.* Being a campaign manager not only involves helping to support a good cause, but also means understanding politics to find new ways to fundraise and gain public support. You could organize a cake sale or create your own online petition to support a cause that you think is important, such as animal rights.

£200

£10

Who's *who?* Some of **the greatest** people in politics were not known as **politicians**, but as philosophers, statesmen, and revolutionaries. While philosophers *wrote* about political theories, leaders put their politics into *practice* – sometimes to huge effect.

CONFUCIUS
551–479 BCE

Confucius was a Chinese philosopher whose ideas influenced the politics of countries in eastern Asia for over 2,000 years. He believed that governments should rule by providing morals to follow rather than setting laws and punishments. Citizens would try to be good and have a sense of shame if they were not. Rulers should lead by moral example and govern with love and concern for all people.

MARCUS CICERO
106–43 BCE

The Roman statesman Cicero is considered the father of constitutionalism and modern law. As the Roman Republic collapsed into civil war, he tried to persuade the divided senate to follow the republican principles of democracy. His speeches and writings have influenced political ideas and shaped constitutions in Europe and the USA. He continues to be the most quoted political writer.

NICCOLO MACHIAVELLI
1469–1527 CE

After being removed from serving as a diplomat for the government of Florence, Italy, Machiavelli turned to political writing. He published a handbook for rulers, called *The Prince*, which stated that governments should be seen as good and compassionate but to act with cunning and ruthlessness. The modern word "Machiavellianism" means to use cunning and deceit in politics.

JEAN-JACQUES ROUSSEAU
1712–1778

In the 18th century, the Swiss philosopher Rousseau went against the idea of progress as he believed this caused unhappiness for people. Instead, society and education should allow individuals to express themselves. He proposed that governments should give freedom, equality, and justice to all citizens. His writings inspired the leaders of the French Revolution, and sparked ideas for modern socialism and communism.

> I have tasted **command**, and I cannot give it up.

> *Deeds, not words.*

NAPOLEON BONAPARTE
1769–1821

The great French military leader Napoleon was involved in a coup d'etat in 1799, established a military dictatorship, and made himself emperor of France in 1802. He centralized the government of France, created the Bank of France, and reformed the law with his Napoleonic Code based on common sense. He conquered much of Europe, but his wars were costly and he began to be defeated. In 1814, he was forced into exile and later imprisoned.

QUEEN VICTORIA
1819–1901

Queen Victoria was ruler of Great Britain and Ireland from 1837 to 1901. During her long reign, known as the "Victorian age", the British Empire expanded and the country industrialized, leading to huge social changes. She restored public respect for royalty, which developed into a constitutional monarchy where the queen had few powers, but was an important figurehead for the country.

EMMELINE PANKHURST
1858–1928

Born into a political family in Manchester, England, Emmeline Pankhurst was a key figure in gaining votes for women in the UK. She founded the Women's Franchise League in 1889 and the Women's Social and Political Union in 1903. Its members, the suffragettes, used violent means to get their cause noticed, including arson, smashing windows, and hunger strikes, and were often arrested.

MAHATMA GANDHI
1869–1948

The Indian political and spiritual leader Gandhi gained respect from the people and had a huge influence over the country's political and social progress. He led campaigns for peaceful protests and non-cooperation against British rule, wanted to end discrimination amongst India's caste system, and argued for education and work for Indians in rural communities. He was assassinated soon after India achieved independence.

Who's *who* too?

> The price of **greatness** is **responsibility**.

> *The people, and the people alone, are the motive force in the making of world history.*

WINSTON CHURCHILL
1874–1965

Sir Winston Churchill is considered one of Britain's greatest prime ministers and politicians. He served twice as prime minister – during World War II, and then from 1951 to 1955. He encouraged the British people through the war with his great speeches and determination to win, and he planned with the other leaders of the Allied forces to gain victory. He was so respected that his funeral was attended by a huge number of world leaders.

CHIANG KAI-SHEK
1887–1975

In 1925, Chiang became leader of the Chinese Nationalist Party, which had overthrown the Qing dynasty in 1911, creating a republic after centuries of emperor-led rule. Using his military experience, Chiang re-unified China and then established a modern Chinese state. He reformed banking, built a transport network, and enforced laws based on Confucius's moral ideas. He fled to Taiwan when the Communist party took control in 1949.

JAWAHARLAL NEHRU
1889–1964

In 1947, Nehru became the first prime minister of independent India after being actively involved in the long struggle for the country's complete independence from British rule. He established a parliamentary government, which oversaw the growth of industry and rural India, the building of schools and colleges, and increased legal rights and freedoms for all. He also worked towards achieving international peace.

MAO ZEDONG
1893–1976

As leader of China's Communist Party, Mao led a revolution to take over the government in 1949. After renaming the country the People's Republic of China, he set about reforming China's industry and agriculture, and carried out a programme to reshape China's society. Many thousands of people died and much of China's cultural history was destroyed, but any opposition was ruthlessly suppressed.

> I dream of an Africa which is in peace with itself.

> *Change will not come if we wait for some other person or some other time. We are the ones we've been waiting for. We are the change that we seek.*

NELSON MANDELA 1918–2013	**CHE GUEVARA** 1928–1967	**MIKHAIL GORBACHEV** 1931–	**BARACK OBAMA** 1961–
Involved with the multi-racial political party the African National Congress (ANC), Nelson Mandela sought to end the apartheid (forced segregation) in South Africa. In 1963, he was imprisoned for life, becoming a symbol of resistance to segregation. After lots of international and internal pressure, the South African government released him in 1990. In 1993 he became president of South Africa, and was also awarded the Nobel Peace Prize.	Argentinean-born Guevara has become an icon of revolutionary change. He travelled around South and Central America and was horrified by the poverty he saw, believing that armed revolution was the only solution. In 1955, Guevara joined Fidel Castro's successful but violent communist campaign to overthrow the dictator Fulgencio Batista during the Cuban Revolution. Guevara was later executed by the Bolivian army.	In 1985, Gorbachev became General Secretary (leader) of the Communist Party of the Soviet Union and began to turn the country into a democracy. He was the last president of the Union of Soviet Socialist Republics (USSR) as his reforms led to the break-up of the Soviet Union in 1991. He also ended the Cold War (a period of rivalry between the USA and the USSR) and was awarded the Nobel Peace Prize in 1990.	As 44th president of the United States of America, Obama is noted for being the first African-American to achieve this position. He was inaugurated (officially started) in January 2009 and has since then dealt with the banks' economic crises and the wars in Iraq and Afghanistan, refreshed relationships between international governments, and is seeking to make healthcare and social reforms for Americans.

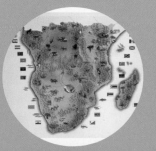

GLOSSARY

"~archy"/ "~cracy" A word ending in ~archy or ~cracy describes a style of government, such as monarchy or democracy.

"~ism" A word ending in ~ism is a name given to a specific set of political ideas, for example capitalism.

absolute monarchy A style of government where the king or queen holds all the political power.

ambassador A messenger sent as a representative from one state to another. Ambassadors today are usually called diplomats.

anarchy "Without rule." An anarchic state has no government.

aristocracy Originally a form of government that meant "rule by the best", today the word usually refers to the upper classes.

authoritarianism When a government imposes lots of control over all parts of society.

authority If someone has authority, it means they have the right to impose their rules onto someone else.

autocracy Any form of government where one person or a small group of people are in charge. They are usually self-appointed.

ballot An individual vote that a citizen uses to elect someone.

Many of these ideas have been the subject of debate.

cabinet A small group of senior politicians in a government. They are usually responsible for areas such as a state's defence, home affairs, and foreign affairs.

capitalism A set of political ideas based on an economic system where people are encouraged to own property and earn their own money.

citizen A person who legally lives in a state and is allowed to participate there (for example, they have the right to work or go to school).

civil society The part of a state that includes businesses, industries, local community groups, and religious organizations – institutions that citizens can have some control over without the government's involvement.

class system A way of describing a person's place in society – they are upper, middle, or lower class.

coalition A team of groups that work together, such as two political parties joining together to run the country.

communism Karl Marx's original idea for communism was the opposite of capitalism – nobody would own private property, but there would be common ownership and everyone would work together equally. In communist states, all property and businesses belong to the state.

confederation A system of government where different local authorities work together to make rules for the country, but keep a lot of sovereignty to rule their own areas.

conservatism A conservative government believes in traditional values and tries to conserve (keep) things the way they are.

constitution A written set of rules of how a state will be governed. It defines the role of the government, the laws of the land, and the rights of the citizens.

constitutional monarchy A state that has a king or queen as a figurehead, but the real political power is set out in a constitution (so the monarch can't suddenly declare new rules).

coup d'etat A sudden, often violent, overthrow of a government, usually by the military.

debate A discussion where two people present arguments agreeing and disagreeing with a motion (the idea or question being discussed) so that other people can vote for or against it.

democracy Originally meaning "rule by the citizens", democracy now means a system of government where people outside the government can have a say in how the state is run, usually through voting.

dictator A person who seizes control of a state and runs it according to his or her own rules, often without caring for the citizens.

diplomacy When states formally talk to each other, perhaps to stop a crisis or to work together.

economy The economy is the part of politics that deals with money. It can cover such things as jobs, development, and how much money a state has to buy things from other states or to fund services for its own citizens.

election A vote to choose who should be in power.

empire A set of lands, sometimes not even near each other, that is ruled over by one government.